CULTURE SMART!
COLOMBIA

Kate Cathey

·K·U·P·E·R·A·R·D·

This book is available for special discounts for bulk purchases for sales promotions or premiums. Special editions, including personalized covers, excerpts of existing books, and corporate imprints, can be created in large quantities for special needs.

For more information in the USA write to Special Markets/Premium Sales, 1745 Broadway, MD 6–2, New York, NY 10019, or e-mail specialmarkets@randomhouse.com.

In the United Kingdom contact Kuperard publishers at the address below.

ISBN 978 1 85733 545 3
This book is also available as an e-book: eISBN 978 1 85733 549 1

British Library Cataloguing in Publication Data
A CIP catalogue entry for this book is available from the British Library

Copyright © 2011 Kuperard
Second printing 2012

First published in Great Britain 2011
by Kuperard, an imprint of Bravo Ltd
59 Hutton Grove, London N12 8DS
Tel: +44 (0) 20 8446 2440   Fax: +44 (0) 20 8446 2441
www.culturesmart.co.uk
Inquiries: sales@kuperard.co.uk

Distributed in the United States and Canada
by Random House Distribution Services
1745 Broadway, New York, NY 10019
Tel: +1 (212) 572-2844   Fax: +1 (212) 572-4961
Inquiries: csorders@randomhouse.com

Series Editor Geoffrey Chesler
Design Bobby Birchall

Printed in Malaysia

Cover image: *Wayuu woven bags on a market stall in Cartagena*
© Dreamstime.com

The photographs on pages 47, 61, 106, 109, 111, and 129 (bottom) are reproduced by permission of the author.

Images on the following pages reproduced under Creative Commons Attribution-Share Alike 3.0 Unported license: 13 © Martin Roca; 15 and 164 © Philipp Weigell; 24 © Shadowxfox; 31 © Fundación Manuel Cepeda Vargas para la Paz, la Justicia Social y la Cultura; 35 © Guillermo Ramos Flamerich; 36 © BankingBum; 40 © Center for American Progress; 44 © (top note) Luifranhedi, Fibonacci (bottom note); 51and 79 © Epm estamos ahi; 57 author not given; 66, 119, 125 (bottom), and 131 © Pedro Felipe; 70 (left) © Etienne Le Cocq; 102 © Rubashkyn; 105 (top) © Leopupy; 105 (bottom), 112 (top), 136, and 142 © Jdvillalobos; 107 and 120 (bottom) © Wikipedia Author F3rn4nd0; 117 © Anoryat; 123 © Pilar Quintana; and 127 © Louise Wolff

Under Creative Commons Attribution-Share Alike 2.0 Generic license: 14 © Julien H; 16 © Ben Bowes; 20 (top) © Gavin Rough; 33 © Marco Suárez; 69 © Steven Joyce; 70 (right) Otto Nassar; 74 © Luis Pérez; 75 © Hilcias Salazar; 91 © by nati_fg; 96 © laloking97; 120 (top) © Turista Perene; 125 (bottom) © Peter; and 130 © carlosfpardo. Under Creative Commons Attribution-Share-Alike 2.5 Generic license: 20 (bottom) © Brunosan; 26 © "Taken by myself"

About the Author

KATE CATHEY is a writer, cultural researcher, and traveler currently based in Bogotá, Colombia. Born in the USA, she attended Sarah Lawrence College in New York, where she studied Art History, and later graduated with a BA in World Arts and Cultures, concentration in Anthropology, from the University of California, Los Angeles. Since then, she has traveled extensively in Latin America, researching and writing about regional cultural and culinary traditions. She has lived in Mexico City, where she attended and wrote about small town *fiestas, ferias,* and festivals throughout the country, and studied indigenous gastronomy and ritual at the Universidad Nacional Autónoma de México. In 2009 Kate moved to Colombia where she continues these pursuits. She also directs cultural travel programs and is a regular contributor to Bogotá's English language newspaper, *The City Paper.*

contents

contents

Map of Colombia

PROVIDENCIA IS.

SAN ANDRÉS IS.

CARIBBEAN SEA

Riohacha

Santa Marta

Barranquilla

Cartagena
El Salado
Valledupar

ROSARIO IS.

DARIEN GULF

Sincelejo

Monteria

PANAMA

Cauca R.

Magdalena R.

Cucuta

VENEZUELA

Bucaramanga

ANDES

Medellin
Nobsa
Villa de Leyva
Mongui

Puerto Carreño

Quibdó
Manizales
Chiquinquiá
Tunja
Yopai

Pereira
Tabio
ANDES

Tolima
Bogotá

PACIFIC
OCEAN

Armenia
Ibague
Villavicencio

Puerto Inirida

Buenaventura
Cali
Palmira
Puerto Tejada
Neiva

Popayán
San José
del Guaviare

Florencia

Mitu

Pasto
Mocoa

ANDES

EQUATOR

ECUADOR

BRAZIL

PERU

Leticia

introduction

People don't really know what to make of Colombia. In the collective imagination, Colombia is the unknown—exotic, lawless, and dangerous. And while the illegal narcotics trade and an ongoing armed conflict have understandably contributed to its bad-boy image, things are changing, and there is much more to it than that.

This is a magical country, full of spectacular landscapes, exotic wildlife and rare ecosystems, succulent tropical fruits, salsa and cumbia music, and kind, fun-loving people. Its landscapes range from jagged Andean peaks, rolling green hills, tropical jungles, white sandy beaches, and thundering waterfalls, to fern forests filled with many unique plant and animal species. Isolated by its rugged topography and by years of violence, many parts of the country have been left untouched, preserving its natural beauty and rich biodiversity.

Colombia is a paradox. In some regions it rains more than 200 inches (5,000 mm) a year, and in others there are arid deserts. Its fertile lands produce much of the world's coffee, tropical fruits, and bananas; yet the majority of Colombians do not enjoy the economic rewards. The major cities are modern, stylish, and cosmopolitan, but a five-minute drive into the countryside reveals a slower, more bucolic past.

As a result of the Spanish conquest, Colombia's modern culture is rich and multiethnic, a synthesis of Spanish, indigenous, and African traditions, evident in the music, the food, and Barranquilla's famous Carnaval. Yet, much of Colombian society ignores this diversity by favoring everything European. Colonization created a strict class system, dividing the people into the upper and lower classes with little chance of social mobility, although in recent years a strong middle class has emerged. As a result of this extreme social inequality, there has been strife— severe political divisions, lawlessness, and discontent that has manifested itself in long-lived insurgent and counter-insurgent movements and a cycle of astounding violence that has saturated four decades with the undeclared civil war that Colombians call "the armed conflict."

Despite so much suffering, the Colombian people have shown a steady dignity. What has happened to them has made them stronger, never sullen or defeated. Still, they are animated, lighthearted, and ready to enjoy the moment. They have found strength in each other, in their families and closest friends.

Culture Smart! Colombia will help you understand the complex and often contradictory nature of the Colombians. It shows how the country's rough geography and tumultuous history have shaped present-day values and attitudes. It describes social customs and traditions, examines life at home with family, and introduces you to some distinct and delicious culinary traditions. You'll learn how Colombians think about each other, their neighbors, and foreigners. There is advice on safe travel, vital information on how business is done, and how Colombians communicate with each other. Ultimately, *Culture Smart! Colombia* will share with you the intricacies of a culture that is both modern and steeped in tradition, international and regional, cosmopolitan and agrarian, very rich and very poor, and after decades of civil war is slowly emerging from the shadow of conflict and getting ready for the future.

Key Facts

Official Name	República de Colombia	Independence from Spain in 1810; Republic in 1823
Capital City	Bogotá, D.C.	Pop. 8,566,926 Altitude: 8,661 feet (2,640 m)
Main Cities	Bogotá, Medellín, Cali, Barranquilla, Cartagena	Over 75% of the population live in four major cities.
Area	440,000 sq. miles (1.14 million sq. km)	4th largest country in South America
Geography	Top NW corner of South America. The equator runs through the Amazon basin in the south.	Shares borders with Panama, Venezuela, Brazil, Peru, and Ecuador
Terrain	Diverse. High alt. mountains, tropical jungles, interior lakes, hot springs; wetlands, prairies, deserts, and tropical beaches	Long coastlines on the Pacific and Caribbean. Two major rivers run south to north: the Rio Magdalena and the Rio Cauca.
Climate	Climate varies with altitude. Cool and dry with rain in the Andes; hot, wet, and humid at lower alts.	Three temp. regions related to alt.: "hot country," "temperate country," and "cold country"
Seasons	Dry and wet seasons. Dry months: Dec, Jan, Feb, June, July, Aug. Wet months: March, April, May, Sept, Oct, Nov.	Due to location near the equator the sun rises and sets around the same time (6:00 a.m. and 6:00 p.m.) every day of the year.
Population	Approx. 45 million	
Life Expectancy	Men: 68 Women: 75	

Ethnic Makeup	58% Mestizo (Amerindian/White), 20% White, 14% Mulatto (Black/White), 4% Afro-Colombian, 3% Zambo (African/Amerindian), 1% Amerindian	
Currency	Colombian peso (COP). The US dollar sign is used.	The decimal point is used in place of a comma in the thousand place, i.e. $3.000 COP.
GDP	US$8,205 per capita per annum	
Language	Spanish	Considered the purest form spoken in Latin America
Religion	90% Roman Catholic 10% other	
Literacy	91.6% in urban areas 67% in rural areas	
Government	Democratic Republic	President serves a four-year term and can be reelected once.
Media	National newspaper: *El Tiempo*. Weekly news magazine: *Semana*	English-language: newspaper, *The City Paper*; online news, *Colombia Reports*
Electricity	110 volts, 60 Hz. European appliances need adapters.	Surge protectors recommended. Outages frequent
Video/TV	NTSC	DVD zone 4
Internet Domain	.co	
Telephone	Colombia's country code is 57. Cities have their own codes.	Landline to cell phone calls require special dialing codes.
Time Zone	EST, with no Daylight Saving	For UK, GMT-5

LAND & PEOPLE

GEOGRAPHY

Colombia sits at the northwest corner of South America, wedged between Ecuador and Venezuela. The fourth-largest country in South America, it enjoys two long coastlines, one on the Pacific Ocean and the other on the Caribbean Sea. The equator runs through Colombia's southern jungles after it passes through Ecuador and on its way to Brazil. Just offshore from the northern coastal city of Cartagena sit the Islas del Rosario, in the Caribbean Sea. Further north off the coast of Nicaragua's Caribbean coast are two palm-lined Colombian islands, Providencia and San Andrés. A speck of Colombia touches Panama to the northwest, once part of Colombian territory. Colombia shares borders with Venezuela to the northeast, Brazil to the southeast, and Peru and Ecuador to the south.

The Andes mountains define Colombia's landscape and have dictated its settlement and development since pre-Hispanic times. Three rugged mountain ranges extend from north to south, dividing the country—the Cordillera Occidental, the Cordillera Central, and the Cordillera Oriental, whose peaks reach above 16,000 feet (5,000 m) in places. Where there are no mountains, there are fertile river valleys and high altitude plateaus, tropical beaches, dense jungle, and the *páramos*: rare high elevation ecosystems consisting of glacier carved valleys, plateaus, lakes, forests, deserts, and wetlands.

To the west of the Cordillera Occidental lies the hot
and humid Pacific coast. To the east the agricultural
lands of the Cauca River Valley feed the *departamento*
of Antioquia and the Zona Cafetera, where Colombia's
famous coffee is grown. The Cordillera Central cuts down
through the center of the country, Colombia's backbone.
The Magdalena River, Colombia's main artery, flows
northward, following the Cordillera Central until it
empties into the ocean at the Caribbean port of
Barranquilla. To the east, the Cordillera Oriental marks
the beginning of Los Llanos de Orinoco, vast grasslands
that stretch all the way to Venezuela and Brazil. To the
south, Colombia's Amazon rain forest reaches into
Ecuador, Peru, and Brazil.

Colombia is stunningly beautiful, with vast regions of
unimaginable biodiversity. On a short trip you can enjoy
snow tipped mountains, green rolling hills, cloudy
highland plateaus, steamy tropical beaches, hot tangled
jungles, emerald lakes, verdant river valleys, and more
than 50 percent of the world's *páramos*. The world's
largest *páramo*, El Páramo de Sumapaz, is only 23 miles
(37 km) outside Bogotá. In these bewildering and unique
ecosystems thrive thousands of endemic species.

Colombia's biodiversity is well documented, boasting 1,880 species of birds, 700 species of amphibians, 400 species of mammals, and 3,500 species of orchids. In Colombia, plant and animal species are still being discovered.

CLIMATE

Although Colombia officially is in the Tropics, between the Tropic of Cancer and the Tropic of Capricorn, not all of Colombia has tropical weather. Colombia's climate varies depending on altitude and rainfall. Chocó, on Colombia's Pacific coast, receives some of the highest levels of annual rainfall in the world, up to 228 inches (6,000 mm) of rain a year! Coastal and jungle areas are hot and humid, while the highland plateau enjoys a milder climate and cooler temperatures.

The country is divided into three temperature zones, the *tierra caliente, tierra templada,* and the *tierra fría.* The hot lands, *tierra caliente,* start at sea level and go up through 3,608 feet (1,100 m). Sitting a little higher are the temperate lands, *tierra templada,* ranging from 3,608 feet to 9,842 feet (1,100 to 3,000 m). Highest and coldest are the cold lands, *tierra fría,* above the tree line.

Most of Colombia's population live in the temperate zone where higher altitudes provide relief from the hot weather of the lowlands. The temperate zone consists of

the Cauca River Valley (around Cali), the Magdalena River Valley (departments of Quindio, Caldas, Tolima, and Cundinamarca), and the Aburra Valley (department of Antioquia), as well as the highland plateau region in and around Bogotá (departments of Cundinamarca and Boyacá). Colombia has experienced mass urbanization over the last forty years due to economic pressures and the ongoing armed conflict. Now, over 70 percent of the population live in urban areas.

Since Colombia is near the equator, temperatures and daylight remain nearly the same all year-long. With minimal variation, the sun rises at 6:00 a.m. and sets at 6:00 p.m. every day of the year. Colombia has typical tropical wet and dry seasons running in three-month cycles. December through February are dry, then March through May are rainy, and so on.

Bogotá's high altitude, 8,661 feet (2,640 m), makes for chilly weather all the year. The city's weather might be like living in constant fall, but it is exciting and dynamic, and Bogotanos say that you can see four seasons in one day. Days typically range between 57 and 66°F (14 and 19°C), with nights falling to 48°F (9°C). It rains an average of 185 days a year in Bogotá so Bogotanos are used to rainy weather and don't let it affect their daily life. When the sky looks dark and threatening you will hear *"Tiene ganas de llover,"* " It really wants to rain

badly," or *"Amenaza lluvia,"* " It is threatening to rain." When a downpour is coming you will hear *"Va a caller un lago de agua,"* "An entire lake of water is going to come down." Make sure to pack your umbrella.

Off the high plateau, Colombia's weather warms up quickly, and at sea level it is truly tropical.

Medellín, northwest of Bogotá at an elevation of 4,905 feet (1,495 m), is considered "the city of eternal spring," where temperatures remain a pleasant 71°F (22°C) during the day and 55°F (13°C) at night, inspiring flowers to bloom perennially. In late July and early August, Paisas (people from Antioquia) celebrate the blooms with the Festival de Las Flores, their annual Flower Festival. In Cartagena, on Colombia's Caribbean coast, days and nights are Caribbean hot—89°F (32°C) during the day and 73°F (23°C) at night. October through May is considered the "high" season, when the heat is accompanied by slightly cooling trade winds. June through September, without that mitigation, it feels even hotter.

COLOMBIA'S DEPARTMENTS

Colombia is a democratic sovereign republic with a central government that delegates certain powers to its departments, similar to states in the USA. Colombia is divided into 32 *departamentos*, or departments, with a capital district in Bogotá. Each department is governed by an elected governor and a department assembly.

Departments are divided further into municipalities, which are governed by a mayor.

Most Colombians live in and around four major cities, Bogotá, Medellín, Cali, and Barranquilla. Small rural villages dot the landscape throughout much of the country when the topography allows. Only 3 percent of the population lives in Colombia's vast southern departments, which make up more than half the area of the country.

Many regions of Colombia are so mountainous or so tangled in jungle that they stay untamed. Much of the southern jungle area along the Ecuadorian and Peruvian borders continues to be lawless and controlled by illegal armed groups and narco-traffickers, a no-go zone for travelers. Many departments, such as Tolima, Valle de Cauca, Meta, and Nariño, are still hot spots in Colombia's forty-five-year armed conflict. Some regions remain untouched by the modern world. In the most southern department of Amazonas, near Leticia, there is said to be an indigenous tribe that has not yet revealed itself to the outside world.

Historically, Colombia's rough terrain has made building infrastructure and moving around the country difficult. Without effective transportation and trade routes, regions remained isolated. Fertile lands and abundant natural resources allowed communities to be self-sufficient. In this environment, distinct cultural identities and a strong sense of regionalism developed and still exists today. Ask a Colombian where he is from, and he will tell you, "I am Antioqueño" (from the department of Antioquia), before he will say, "I am Colombian."

THE PEOPLE

Colombia's 45 million people are a multiethnic group. Almost 80 percent of the population is of mixed race, diversity resulting from Spanish colonization and slavery.

Today more than half, about 58 percent, of the population is mestizo, a mix of native Amerindians and Spanish Europeans, while 20 percent are of pure European descent. Even though Europeans have been the minority, they have held the power since colonial times.

Afro-Colombians, descendants of African slaves brought to Colombia by the Spanish to work in the gold mines, and Colombia's indigenous peoples have traditionally held the lowest positions in society, and experience the most discrimination. Most of the Afro-Colombian population settled along the Pacific and Caribbean coasts, where some 14 percent of the population is mulatto (black mixed with white Europeans), 4 percent Afro-Colombian, and 3 percent Zambo (African mixed with Amerindian.) An estimated 90 percent of the population of the department of Chocó is black. Only 1 percent of Colombia's indigenous population remains today, and are among the most affected by the continuing armed conflict.

Of course, Colombia's first immigrants were Spanish, but small numbers of European groups immigrated in the 1940s during the Second World War. Colombia has not experienced the same degree of immigration as Argentina or Venezuela, due to economic and security issues, but there has been some. The largest immigrant population comes from nearby Venezuela, followed by the USA and Ecuador, closely followed by Peru, Argentina, and Mexico. Immigrants of Arab descent—Lebanese, Syrian, and Palestinian—have settled on the Caribbean coast. The Romani "gypsy" population is prominent in many cities. There are German areas of Santander where it is common to see blonde-haired, blue-eyed peasants. Small populations of Spanish, French, Italian, British, and Chinese have also settled in Colombia. Former presidential candidate and two-time mayor of Bogotá Antanas Mockus is the son of Lithuanian immigrants.

A BRIEF HISTORY

Colombia's history has been a violent one, an endless conflict over lack of equality, social justice, power, and money. It has also been convoluted and confusing, with rebels becoming political leaders, and it is hard to separate the good guys from the bad. After Simón Bolívar liberated Colombia from Spanish rule, his ideas of social equality were quickly forgotten. In the newly independent Colombia not much changed. Society remained highly stratified, the heirs of the Spanish remained at the top of society, and most everyone else fell to the bottom.

In this rigid class system the disparity between the haves and the have-nots was enormous, with extreme wealth countered by extreme poverty. Frustration spawned a renegade tradition of outlaws, *banditos,* guerrillas, and militias that have been at the core of Colombia's armed conflict. The roots of lawlessness and violence run deep. The untamable terrain and the independent nature of the people have made it difficult to govern. Since the colonial period, no leader has been able to completely unify the country and its people.

Indigenous Groups

When the Spanish first set foot on Colombian soil in the sixteenth century, they encountered numerous nomadic and agricultural tribes, some hunter-gatherers, others subsistence farmers. Some were talented goldsmiths and artisans, others great engineers and builders.

At the time of the Spanish conquest, Colombia's indigenous inhabitants were not as populous or as developed as the great civilizations of Mexico and Peru, largely due to the constraints of the terrain. These were the San Augustíns—considered somewhat of a mystery and known for the giant carved stone figures they left behind—and the Chibchas. Of the many Chibcha tribes, historians know most about the Taironas and the Muiscas.

The Taironas made their home at the lower elevations of the isolated Sierra Nevada de Santa Maria, the mountains that rise up above Santa Marta on the northern Caribbean coast. They appear to be the only precolonial Colombians to achieve real urban civilization, and are known as the builders and engineers of the urban complex of La Ciudad Perdida (The Lost City) that dates from 800 CE.

The Muiscas were less creative than the Taironas, but far outnumbered them. They are thought to be the largest indigenous group, topping 600,000 at the time of the Spanish conquest. Farmers and weavers, they cultivated corn and potatoes in the fertile Sabana de Bogotá soil.

One thing we do know is that the native Colombians had a fondness for gold. Some mined it from their own lands, and those who could not acquired it through trade.

They became excellent goldsmiths, modeling elaborate jewelry, ceremonial vessels, and even ceremonial clothes hammered from glittering sheets of gold. Today Colombia has very few communities of unassimilated native peoples. The Spanish quickly wiped out most of the native Colombians through disease and conquest, and easily assimilated most of the rest.

Without searching, the regular tourist to Colombia won't feel the indigenous presence because most exist in remote areas, many in the Amazon jungle. The remaining native peoples have been severely affected by years of armed conflict and the narcotics trade. The Nukak Makú, Colombia's last nomadic tribe, numbering about six hundred, have been displaced from their jungle territory in the department of Guaviare by years of cocaine trafficking and fighting, and now face an uncertain future, while the Guambiano people in the department of Cauca have also suffered from guerrilla and narcotics trade violence.

THE LEGEND OF EL DORADO

The Muiscas mined salt, not gold. But they had a passion for the shimmering nuggets, and traded their precious salt for the precious metal. The legend of *El Dorado*, "The Gilded Man," is believed to come from a Muisca ceremony. To install the new chief and assure balance to the spiritual world, the incoming chief would cover himself in gold dust, ride on an ornately decorated raft to the center of Lake Guatavita, 35 miles (56 km) northeast of Bogotá, then throw himself into the cold waters, along with piles of gold jewelry and trinkets, carvings, and emeralds, as offerings to appease the gods. When he emerged from the waters, the gold dust from his body and the other precious offerings had fallen to the bottom of the lake. The gods were considered satisfied and he was officially declared the new chief. Bogotá's impressive Museo del Oro has an extensive collection of indigenous gold work, including many pieces recovered from Lake Guatavita.

Colonial Colombia

The Spanish arrived on Colombian shores in the early 1500s. Within thirty years they had permanent settlements along the Caribbean coast, first in Santa Marta, then in Cartagena. By 1536, explorers were pushing inland in search of riches. Lured by talk of wealthy kingdoms and tales of El Dorado, three independent Spanish expeditions were working their way toward the interior of Colombia, all from different directions.

From Venezuela, Nicolás Federmann crossed over the empty, barren, and often flooded Llanos grasslands towards Muisca territory. Sebastián de Benalcázar forged north from Ecuador into Colombia through the Amazon jungle, laying claim to Popayán and Cali along the way. But when Federmann and Benalcázar reached Muisca territory, they found Gonzalo Jiménez de Quesada already there.

Quesada had set off from Santa Maria with eight hundred men in search of the famed golden kingdoms. On the way to the highlands Quesada lost most of his men, to disease, starvation, and exhaustion. With only two hundred men left he finally made it to the interior, where they found the Muiscas living on fertile lands, harvesting corn and potatoes, and decorating their houses with gold leaf ornaments. Quesada's men were delighted, easily subdued the Muiscas, and made off with large amounts of gold. In 1538 Quesada declared Bogotá the new Spanish capital of the conquered lands, which he named New Granada after his hometown in Spain.

The Spanish were consumed by their quest for gold. They were convinced the Muiscas had vast gold mines, which, in fact, they did not. The Spanish did, however, end up finding substantial quantities of gold in Colombia. Under colonial rule, gold was the country's main export. Historians often say that Colombia was a disappointment to the Spanish, and indeed their gold output never equaled the great amount of silver that Peru and Mexico produced.

But Colombia was profitable for Spain, producing more gold than any other colony in the Spanish empire.

As in all their other colonies in Latin America, the Spanish needed native labor to make the colony profitable. In Colombia, they put the natives to work in the mines and fields under what they called the *encomienda* system. The natives "worked" for the Spanish in exchange for room and board and a small salary that was paid back to the Crown in the form of taxes. Effectively, the landholders owned the natives and held them in a type of slavery.

The native population were overworked and under-nourished, and vanished quickly. This left a void in the labor force, which the Spanish filled by bringing slaves from Africa to supplement the workforce in the fields and mines. Cartagena was the primary port and the center of the slave trade in Colombia. Today most of the population along the Caribbean and Pacific coasts are descended from former slaves who, over time, mixed with indigenous Colombians and *criollos* (Spanish born in Colombia), giving the Caribbean coast its distinct cultural flavor.

Independence and El Libertador

Almost every Colombian town has a Plaza Simón Bolívar, Parque Bolívar, or Calle Bolívar, a tribute to El Libertador, "The Liberator." Soldier, leader, revolutionary, and hero, Venezuelan born Símon Bolívar (1783–1830) led the armies that freed Colombia—along with Venezuela, Panama, Ecuador, Peru, and Bolivia—from Spanish rule in the early 1800s. Today Bolívar is both a national hero and an ideal. His name represents a united South America that is egalitarian and fair.

Ideas of independence and an opportunity to achieve it rose from two events on two continents. The first was the Revolt of the Comuneros of New Granada, when in 1781 angry criollos and mestizos, outraged over the new taxes, rioted and took control of local towns, setting up their own town councils. These acts set the stage for revolution in Colombia.

The second event was something that was happening in Spain. In 1808 Napoleon dethroned Ferdinand VII, the king of Spain, and tried to install his own brother as the new king. The Spanish people protested, proclaimed their allegiance to Ferdinand, and set up a temporary government, a junta, to resist Napoleon's claims.

With the Spanish king deposed, the subjects of Colombia realized no one was in charge. The Spanish Crown had lost control of its American colonies. Like the Spanish in Spain, Spanish Americans also proclaimed loyalty to Ferdinand and began setting up their own juntas declaring allegiance to him. Ostensibly the juntas would run things in the name of the king until order was restored in Spain. While Spain was preoccupied with its own problems, however, the colonies realized that their time had come. They had tasted freedom and were not going back under Spanish control.

New Granada (modern-day Colombia) declared independence from Spain in 1810, and finally won it in 1819, when Simón Bolívar decisively defeated the Spanish army at Boyacá, his finest military moment. That same year the former territories of the Viceroyalty of New Granada liberated from Spanish rule were united as one independent country, Gran Colombia, which encompassed modern-day Colombia, Ecuador, Panama, and Venezuela, and parts of Central America, Peru, Guyana, and Brazil.

The task of unifying and governing Gran Colombia was doomed from the start, given the size of the new territory and other inherent weaknesses. By 1830, Bolívar's ideal state had splintered into three nations: Colombia, Ecuador, and Venezuela. Though Bolívar ultimately failed to keep Gran Colombia together, he is still a hero to the countries he liberated.

Liberals and Conservatives

Politics and religion were at the center of Colombia's very first struggles as an independent nation, a foreshadowing of things to come. From the beginning independent Colombia was divided into two camps: the Federalists and the Centralists. From these emerged Colombia's two political parties, the Liberals and the Conservatives, who immediately vied for control. Rivalries festered and violence erupted.

The Conservatives aligned themselves with the Roman Catholic Church and the wealthy landowners. The Church aligned itself with the Conservatives, directly involving itself in politics. Under Conservative control, Church and State were one.

The Liberals represented the middle sectors of society, the professional and the merchant classes. Although these sectors were also Catholics, they wanted the separation of Church and State, less power for the Church, more power for the departments, and less for Bogotá. Mainly, there was little difference between the two groups, but people vehemently identified themselves with one side or the other, a "taking sides" mentality that would show its face many times throughout Colombian history.

The Conservatives and the Liberals wrestled power back and forth in a violent cycle that continued throughout the nineteenth century, during which they fought eight civil wars, leaving more than 200,000 dead.

By the 1930s and 1940s the political situation had unraveled further, revealing deep distrust between members of the two parties. In Colombia politics were personal.

El Nueve de Abril—El Bogotazo

To his supporters, Liberal Party leader Jorge Eliécer Gaitán (1903–48) represented a new beginning for Colombia—hope for social equality. He was a magnetic speaker and an intellectual who could move in elite political circles while his mixed blood, indigenous features, and direct approach made him appeal to regular Colombians. He was a voice for change and people worshiped him.

On April 9, 1948, during the Ninth Inter-American Conference held in Bogotá, Jorge Eliécer Gaitán died from a single gunshot on a Bogotá street. His death

plunged the country into darkness, with his supporters taking to the streets in protest. There was mass rioting, looting, drunkenness, destruction, and killing. Liberals blamed the Conservatives for the assassination, and years of political hatred bled to the surface. Much of Bogotá burned to the ground while similar violence occurred all over the country. In Puerto Tejada, south of Cali, Liberals killed Conservatives, decapitated the bodies, and kicked their heads around the main plaza in a gruesome game of soccer.

La Violencia

In Colombia, revenge rooted in partisan hatred has continued in an endless cycle of violence in which the score is never settled. Along the way the reasons for the fighting seem to have been forgotten, but it continues nevertheless. Throughout history Colombians have carried on long-standing *culebras*—family feuds and political rivalries that continue for generations.

Colombians have never figured out a way to heal their wounds. The social, political, and economic divide that existed under colonial rule still festers today: deep feelings of anger and disenfranchisement resurfaced in La Violencia and continue to fuel the current guerrilla and paramilitary conflict.

Liberals, devastated and enraged by Gaitán's murder, set out to settle the score, killing any Conservatives who crossed their path. The Conservatives proved even more ruthless, training *pájaros* (birds) to kill Liberals, skilled assassins who killed brutally and disappeared quickly, like a bird in flight. Killing became a recognized profession. Bodies were mutilated and left in signature positions, as warnings.

The twenty years of violence and bloodshed that followed is known as La Violencia, simply The Violence. The killing between the Liberals and the Conservatives left between 100,000 and 200,000 people dead. Hope for a peaceful future had died with Gaitán.

The National Front

To stop the carnage, General Gustavo Rojas Pinilla took over the government in a military coup. Pinilla's dictatorship was overthrown five years later and a democratic government was put into place. As a sign of political reconciliation, in 1957 the Conservatives and the Liberals signed a peace agreement called the Frente Nacional, the National Front. The two parties agreed to share all government positions equally, and to alternate power in presidential elections.

The National Front mandated a bipartisan system, outlawing new political parties and essentially banning any alternative voice. It did, however, calm the traditional political rivalries and brought La Violencia to an end.

Real economic and social progress was made by the National Front through modernization and urbanization, infrastructure and road construction, education and literacy, exports, civil liberties, and women's and religious rights. But these advances did not reach the rural population and there was still extreme inequality between the social classes. The cycle of violence would continue, only new forms of violence would replace the old.

The Ongoing Armed Conflict

"God made Colombia so beautiful, so rich in natural resources and so spectacular in every way that it was unfair to the rest of the world. So, God evened the score. He populated Colombia with the most evil race of men."

Colombian saying

In 1965, President Guillermo Valencia passed "state of siege" legislation that made it legal to arrest anyone who was "altering the peaceful development of social society." In essence, the government could legally arrest anyone who voiced dissent, demonstrated, protested, participated in a strike, or criticized the government.

Soon dissidents, intellectuals, students, and angry *campesinos* (peasants) began to form rebel groups and take up arms. The FARC, ELN, and M-19 were the largest of the many rebel groups that emerged. The government considered protesters to be the *"braso desarmado"* or "unarmed wing" of the guerrillas, and punished criticism with strong-arm tactics that left even more Colombians disenfranchised. Poor economic times worsened social inequalities, which fueled more discontent.

The leftist guerrillas and right-wing paramilitary groups that formed in response have now been fighting each other and the Colombian government in an undeclared civil war for more than forty years. Innocent victims have "disappeared," been caught in the cross fire, killed, or forced from their villages. Left-wing guerrilla groups have targeted Colombian national infrastructure, major foreign installations, government officials, judges, journalists, indigenous communities, and entire towns. And right-wing groups, who fight the guerrillas, have done worse.

FARC (Fuerzas Armadas Revolucionarias de Colombia)

The Fuerzas Armadas Revolucionarias de Colombia, or Revolutionary Armed Forces of Colombia, founded in 1965 by Pedro Marín, remains the strongest rebel group in the western hemisphere. The FARC claim to be the "people's army," representing the rural poor in their class struggle against Colombia's elite, and say they oppose US intervention in Colombia, multinational corporations, and the privatization of natural resources. At its peak in 2001, the FARC was 16,000 strong, but 2009 figures were down to an estimated 8,500 fighters, mostly children under the age of nineteen, many of them young women.

Pedro Antonio Marín grew up during the 1940s in a Liberal family in a rural Liberal town, where he witnessed the atrocities of La Violencia firsthand. As a Liberal he and his family were targeted by Conservatives, who were killing any Liberals that they could find. With no grand political proclamations he gathered together a band of angry peasants like himself and took up whatever arms were in reach and fought back. Over time, Marín formulated a redistributive agenda, named his rebel group the FARC, and went to war with the government. Marín spent his entire adult life, over forty years, as a guerrilla fighter, better known as Manuel Marulanda Vélez.

In the beginning the FARC financed their revolutionary fight with the help of rural communities, who supplied food, shelter, and medical attention. The guerrillas became the heroes of the countryside, fighting the rich in the name of the poor. Today the FARC fund their activities to the tune of US$500–600 million a year from their involvement in the illegal narcotics trade, coupled with kidnapping and extortion, and enforce their demands with explosives—bombing Bogotá restaurants, clubs, government installations, and local businesses, killing many over the years and instilling fear in residents. Since 2008 a number of blows have weakened the FARC. The deaths of founder Manuel Marulanda Vélez, second-in-command Raul Reyes, and Marin's replacement Mono Jojoy severely impaired the FARC leadership, causing mass defections.

ELN—Ejército de Liberación Nacional

The ELN is the smaller of the leftist guerrilla groups, with about 2,000–3,000 fighters today. Like the FARC, the ELN emerged in 1963 as a direct result of La Violencia. Founder Fabio Vásquez Castaño says he started the ELN to avenge the death of his father, who was killed by Conservative *pájaros*. He recruited angry students, intellectuals, Cuban trained revolutionaries, and a few radical Catholic priests who took up arms and fought in response to Colombia's social inequities—against extreme poverty and exploitation of the masses by the wealthy elite.

M-19—Movimiento de 19 de Abril

M-19 was the urban counterpart to the rural based FARC. They fought their revolution in the cities and slums using urban advertising campaigns as well as armed assaults to make their point. Like the FARC, they fought against the gross inequities in Colombian society.

M-19 members were city slickers—young, hip, and sophisticated. They were educated students and intellectuals who, in the end, were not cut out to be rebel fighters. Their last and most infamous offensive took place in November 1985, when they seized the Palace of Justice in Bogotá's main plaza, taking an estimated 350 people hostage and killing fifty-five of them. The Colombian army and the National Police surrounded the building and entered in armored tanks, killing at least thirty guerrillas, ultimately marking the end of M-19. The rebels surrendered and struck a deal with the government—weapons in exchange for legitimacy. M-19 became an official political party, the government "rewarding terrorism with legitimacy."

Paramilitaries and the AUC (Autodefensas Unidas de Colombia)

In the fight against the FARC and other guerrilla groups the Colombian military was undertrained and overstretched. During the 1960s, under the command of General Alberto Ruiz Novoa, they put "Plan Lazo" into effect, encouraging rural civilians to form armed self-defense groups and become "informants" for the military. These self-defense forces later morphed into the paramilitaries—illegal right-wing armies that fought the guerrillas with the tacit support of the Colombian military—both perpetrating atrocities along the way. The paramilitaries became secret killing squads, conducting mass murders and wiping out entire towns that they accused of being sympathetic to the guerrillas.

Carlos Castaño says he started his paramilitary army to protect good people like himself, *"gente de bien,"* who were tired of the abuses the guerrillas were committing. His sole purpose became revenge, "to find the kidnappers [who had kidnapped and killed his father] among the guerillas." In 1997, Castaño united counterinsurgency paramilitary groups in the Autodefensas Unidas de Colombia, the United Colombian Self-Defense Forces. Ultimately they would control most of northern Colombia. Castaño, who comes from a family of drug traffickers, quickly linked the AUC to the narcotics trade. At one time, the AUC earned 70 percent of their revenues from cocaine related funds.

In 2003, peace talks began with the Uribe government that led to the demobilization of more than 31,000 AUC fighters in 2006. Yet many fighters refused to demobilize and have formed new illegal armed groups.

Paramilitary Demobilization and Justice and Peace
To implement the paramilitary demobilization process (2003–06), the Colombian government passed the Justice and Peace Law in 2005 "to assist victims, ensure justice, and restore the truth" in the largest justice and peace effort in the world. Under the law, paramilitaries who confess all of their crimes, surrender all ill-gotten goods, and cease all criminal activity receive lenient treatment in the form of, for example, greatly reduced jail sentences. If they fail to comply with all of the requirements, the law stipulates that they are removed from the program, are considered criminals, and face full jail sentences for their crimes, including human rights violations and war crimes.

As of 2010, there had been no convictions under the law. Understandably, critics see this as a failure of the process. Yet, under the law, when a conviction takes place the confession process ends, and victims and lawyers can no longer question the convicted. Therefore, some see the lack of convictions as a way of keeping the confession process active, a continuation of the truth being told.

The numbers alone say that the Justice and Peace process is making real progress: victims are discovering the truth and receiving monetary reparations from the government. In 2009 the Colombian government paid victims the equivalent of US$100 million and set aside another US$150 million in 2010 for additional reparations. As a result of confessions, more than 40,000 acts of violence were revealed, including more than 37,000 homicides, and as of 2010, more than 53,000 people affiliated with paramilitary or guerrilla groups demobilized, of which 60 percent were the results of the peace accords with the AUC. Voluntary confessions have led to the recovery of the remains of more than 3,100 murder victims. In addition, as of June 2010, Justice and Peace Investigations resulted in about 500 political leaders and public officials being investigated for links to the paramilitaries or leftist guerrilla groups, some charged with war crimes and genocide.

Although the Justice and Peace Law has been criticized for granting impunity or outright amnesty to criminals guilty of heinous crimes, many view the process as a real effort by the Colombian government to make things right—to find the truth and give reparations to victims.

LA MASACRE DE EL SALADO

What happened at Los Montes de Maria, in the community of El Salado, exemplifies the senseless violence and brutality that infected Colombia and has left millions of innocent victims in its wake. On February 16, 2000, accusing the townspeople of aiding the FARC leftist guerrillas, paramilitary fighters unleashed a punishment on a town that spun horribly out of control.

Over six days, 450 paramilitaries tortured and killed 61 people. Headed by Carlos Castaño, the paramilitary army went on a killing spree. First they rounded up the townspeople in the town plaza. Then they strangled and stabbed them. They stabbed a woman while others raped her. They killed a pregnant woman. They cut off people's ears. While they killed they celebrated—played music, howled, and danced. As they marched the victims to their deaths, they pounded a death drum, taunting and terrifying them.

Nine years later only 15 of the 450 participants had been charged with a crime. Castaño himself admitted taking part in the massacre, yet has never faced charges. Victims question how 450 paramilitary fighters could have carried out the six-day-long attack without the complicity of others, and of the navy, which was officially patrolling the area. The victims of the massacre of El Salado requested collective reparations from the government but this was denied. When some of the survivors attempted to return to their lands, these had been sold off. They now are part of the *desplacados*, the estimated 3.5 million people who have been forced from their lands as a result of the armed conflict.

"Farclandia"

There have been numerous
negotiation attempts between the
FARC and the government. In the
1980s, as part of the peace process,
FARC members were allowed to
form their own political party, the
UP, Unión Patriótica, now extinct.
Presidential candidate Andrés
Pastrana made negotiations the
cornerstone of his campaign. In 1999, after winning office,
he opened peace talks with the FARC, hoping to put an
end to the violence. As a sign of good faith, he ceded a
section of southern Colombia to the FARC. It was a daring
move, signaling that he was serious about the possibilities
of peace. FARC were handed their own mini-country to
govern as they wished. The capital of their territory, in
the department of Caquetá, became known as Farclandia.

Pastrana believed in negotiations, saying that an
imperfect peace was better than no peace at all. So,
sporadic peace talks sputtered on for three years. The
FARC's victory was shortlived. During that time FARC
violence exploded exponentially. An army official
described the offensive the FARC launched throughout
Colombia as "the largest and most demented guerilla
offensive in the past forty years." Observers were baffled.
When, in 2002, the FARC hijacked a commercial aircraft
and kidnapped a Colombian senator from the plane,
Pastrana ended the peace talks immediately and sent the
armed forces in to recover the ceded territory. Ultimately
Pastrana sacrificed his presidency for the possibility of
peace. Farclandia was an embarrassment and a failure.

Operation Jaque—Colombia's Great Hostage Rescue

In July 2008, the Colombian military pulled off a
remarkable rescue mission. No guns were fired and no

blood was shed. Instead, the military outsmarted the FARC. Operation Jaque (Checkmate) went off so smoothly that neither the FARC nor their hostages knew it was happening.

In March 2008 Colombian intelligence operatives sensed fragmentation and weakness in the FARC leadership after the deaths of both their founder Manuel Marulanda and second-in-command Raul Reyes.

Undercover intelligence agents penetrated the FARC's governing body, and convinced FARC Comandante Cesar to transfer fifteen hostages to another camp. Military operatives posing as FARC guerrillas landed their helicopter in the FARC-controlled southern department of Guaviare, subdued the guerrilla guards, and flew the hostages to freedom.

Among the freed hostages were former presidential candidate French-Colombian Ingrid Betancourt, who was held for six years, eleven former members of the Colombian armed forces, and three US contractors, who were held for more than five years. The flawless rescue was demoralizing for the FARC.

Cocaine and Pablo Escobar

Colombians love their outlaws, the independent rebels who fight for the common man against the establishment. And they respect the self-made man. Pablo Escobar—Colombia's most famous outlaw—was both.

Escobar built perhaps the most powerful cocaine trafficking network in the world from nothing but bravado and brute strength. He ran his business the mafia way, with bribes or bullets, *plata o plomo* (silver or lead). He amassed astounding wealth buying raw coca from Peru and Bolivia, processing it into pure cocaine in Medellín laboratories, then smuggling it into the USA to be sold for gargantuan profits.

It is impossible to escape Colombia's association with cocaine. Escobar and his crew turned Medellín into Colombia's cocaine capital and in the 1980s everyone felt the effects. Cocaine dollars built narco-malls, narco-schools, bars, discos, and narco-mansions, transforming Medellín into a sparkling cosmopolitan city.

Donating millions to local charities, building schools, and constructing low-income housing in the slums of Medellín, Escobar became a champion of the working class. His Medellín Cartel operated in plain sight, buying off local officials and police to make operations run smoothly.

Ultimately Escobar's Medellín Cartel controlled most of the cocaine trade in Colombia, supplying the USA's increasing demand for the white powder and bringing billions of dollars into the country's economy. In 1989, *Forbes* magazine named him the seventh-richest man in the world. Around the same time, *Time* magazine called Medellín "The most dangerous city." With illegal drug trafficking came violence.

The Medellín Cartel kidnapped, killed, and bombed to stay on top. They unleashed terror on Bogotá in the 1990s in a series of kidnappings and bombing in an effort to pressure the government to abandon an extradition treaty with the USA. Among the dead

were famous Colombian journalist Diana Turbay and the 107 passengers of Colombia's domestic Avianca flight 203.

In 1991, as the Colombian government tried to crack down on the illegal trade in the "drug war," an estimated 6,500 people were killed in that year alone.

Pablo Escobar became so powerful and his violent network so vast that both the Colombian and US governments saw him as a threat to Colombia's stability. In 1989 Colombia's president Virgilio Barco asked the US administration for help. Together the two governments implemented a plan to stop Escobar. With the help of US Special Forces, the Colombian government hunted him down. Like any good outlaw, he died a bloody death at the hands of his enemies. After a long hunt in 1993 that put Escobar on the run and rendered his Medellín Cartel a shambles, he was gunned down by the Colombian police on a rooftop of his Medellín hideout. But despite great efforts, the illegal drug trade is still going strong today.

GOVERNMENT

Colombia is a representative democracy with a strong history of civilian elected governments and regular democratic elections. As we have seen, only once in Colombia's history has there been a military coup—when General Gustavo Rojas Pinilla (1953–57) took power to put an end to La Violencia. His dictatorship was eventually overthrown by the Colombian military. A democratic government was reinstituted, and the two main political parties, the Liberals and the Conservatives, were formed.

The government is a three-branch system, with power divided between the executive, legislative, and judicial branches. The president is the chief of the executive branch. The legislature is composed of the Senate and the House of Representatives, who each serve a four-year term. Members of both chambers are elected by popular vote. The 102-member Senate is composed of 100 senators elected from a national candidate list, and two senators elected from a special list reserved for indigenous and Afro-Colombian communities. The 166-member Chamber of Representatives is composed of two representatives for each department and additional representatives according to population, plus four special representatives: two for the Afro-Colombian community, and one each for indigenous, other minorities, and Colombian citizens living abroad.

The president until recently had been limited to one four-year term. President Alvaro Uribe proposed an extension of presidential power to include a second term and was reelected to office with a remarkable 62 percent of the vote. At the end of his two terms Uribe supporters proposed a referendum to allow the president to be reelected to three consecutive terms, which was denied by the Constitutional Court. Uribe's graceful acceptance of the decision was widely recognized as strong democracy at work in Colombia.

Colombia had a two-party system for most of its political history. While the Liberal and Conservative parties still exist, now new and increasingly powerful political parties have come on to the scene. Uribe was a Conservative, but ran for president as an Independent. The Partido Social de Unidad Nacional (Social Party of National Unity), called the Partido de la "U" for short, was formed to unify supporters of Uribe and support his presidency, and is currently Colombia's largest political party. Then there are Liberal party splinter groups, including Cambio Radical (Radical Change), and the Partido Verde (Green Party), as well as the controversial PIN (Partido de Integracion Nacional) party.

There are four high courts, the Constitutional Court, the Supreme Court, the Superior Judiciary Council, the Council of State, and numerous lower courts. Judicial power has historically been weak.

The influence of narco-wealth and the reach of paramilitary and guerrilla threats have infiltrated the judicial system, putting into question the independence of judges and lawyers. US Department of State human rights reports charge Colombia with a historically "inefficient judiciary who are subject to intimidation."

In the presidential elections of 2010, Juan Manuel Santos won with an overwhelming mandate. Santos is seen as Uribe's successor, and is expected to continue his focus on security.

COLOMBIA TODAY
Security

Colombia's last president (2002–10), Alvaro Uribe, ran for office during the height of the conflict between leftist guerrillas, right-wing paramilitary groups, and narco-trafficking interests. During the 1990s and early 2000s Colombia was under siege. Kidnappings, armed attacks, and terrorist attacks were commonplace. Uribe promised the Colombian people to bring security back to the country. He was no stranger to violence. Guerillas had tried to kill him while he was mayor of Antioquia, and there were three attempts on his life during his presidential campaign. The FARC had gunned down his father years before. After winning the

presidency, he put a comprehensive political, economic, and military strategy in place to fight the guerrillas.

Many credit Uribe with significantly decreasing violence in Colombia. As we have seen, he reduced the numbers of guerrilla fighters and oversaw the demobilization of over 31,000 right-wing paramilitary fighters.

Because of policies put in place by Uribe, armed attacks decreased by 91 percent and terrorist attacks by 79 percent. Colombia's larger and highly trained armed forces are now respected and effective. Uribe's efforts have pushed much of the fighting to the remote provinces, giving urban areas like Bogotá a respite from years of terror.

Parapolitics and *El Voto Amarrado*
Paramilitary groups have had their hands in Colombian politics for years. They have selected and funded candidates to run for office, then pressured voters to "tie" their vote to a particular candidate: *"el voto amarrado,"* "the tied vote." In the 2006 10 Congress, the "parapolitics scandal" was exposed. Investigations revealed voter irregularities, such as entire areas voting for the same candidate, and records of regular contact between elected officials and paramilitary leaders, leading to investigations of 35 percent of members of the elected Congress.

The parapolitics scandal landed many politicians from various parties in jail, and left the political party AND (Alianza Democratica Nacional) in ruins. Despite the scandal and the resulting investigations, paramilitary presence in politics surfaced again during the 2010 congressional elections. The remains of the AND party formed a new political party, PIN, running candidates with paramilitary ties, mainly spouses and family members of jailed paramilitary politicians, preserving the political power their fathers and uncles had won during the first scandal.

Plan Colombia
The USA joined forces with Colombia to combat the illegal drug trade that has fed the leftist insurgency and other illegal armed groups with Plan Colombia.

According to the US Department of State, 90 percent of the cocaine that crosses into the USA is processed in Colombia. Under Plan Colombia, the US has sent billions of dollars to Colombia to fund security and counter-narcotics programs, including interdiction efforts, eradication of coca crops and cocaine production facilities, comprehensive police and military training, supplying military equipment and development assistance including alternative development programs, and justice sector reform.

Plan Colombia funds have helped the Colombian government shape a strong and effective military and national police force, through increased numbers and extensive soldier training programs.

Yet, in other ways, Plan Colombia has not met its benchmark goals to reduce cultivation, processing, and distribution of illegal narcotics. Critics maintain that Plan Colombia's shortcomings are due to its heavy military focus. They believe the plan should concentrate less on eradication and uprooting of crops, and more on alternative economic development for rural communities where coca is the current crop of choice.

Poverty Today

Not everyone is benefiting from the 2001–07 boom years or the 2009–10 surge in direct foreign investment in the oil and mining sectors. Colombia's poor are becoming poorer while the rich are getting richer. During the same boom years Brazil, Peru, and Ecuador have cut their poverty level by double digits, whereas Colombia's reduction has been much less, even while the GDP continued to rise. The quality of life for urban Colombians has improved significantly, but these benefits are not reaching the people that need them most. Even in the midst of the prosperity of 2010, Colombia's unemployment rate was 12 percent.

One reason for high unemployment and growing poverty is the failure to create new jobs, forcing more people into informal employment, street vending, and illegal activities. Another factor is the rising needs of the estimated 3.5 million displaced people, fallout from the armed conflict, a uniquely Colombian problem in the region. While the rest of South America is making great advances in reducing poverty, Colombia has joined the list of countries with the worst poverty in the world.

Human Rights

While Uribe made advances in security, prosperity, and education, a number of military scandals, government cover ups, and civil rights failures came to light during his administration. The DAS (Departamento Administrativo de Seguridad) was investigated for planting false evidence to manipulate elections, committing information crimes, and illegally wiretapping civilians. As noted before, numerous senators are being investigated for links with paramilitary groups. As many as 1,300 Colombian security force members are being investigated in the "false positives" scandal, which involves more than 2,300 victims of extrajudicial executions in which members of the security forces murdered civilians and claimed them as guerrilla casualties.

The US State Department cited numerous government human rights abuses committed in 2009. These included unlawful and extrajudicial killings of civilians, corruption, insubordinate military collaboration with terrorist groups, forced disappearances, impunity and an inefficient judiciary subject to intimidation, illegal surveillance of civilian groups, political opponents and torture of detainees, as well as the intimidation and harassment of journalists. Still, the State Department notes improvements in the human rights situation, including increased security, decreased terrorist activity, a dramatic reduction of extrajudicial killings, and an increase of confessions of former AUC members as part of the Justice and Peace process. Human Rights groups have urged the Obama administration to hold out on confirming the US Free Trade Agreement with Colombia until Colombia addresses human rights offenses.

THE ECONOMY

Colombia's free market economy has remained remarkably stable in light of the global economic downturn and the internal armed conflict, outperforming most of the countries of Latin America. Colombia has the fifth-largest economy in Latin America; its GDP has grown steadily from 2001 to 2007, and it is currently experiencing a surge in direct foreign investment in oil and mining. There have been no major currency devaluations or periods of hyperinflation. In the 1990s President Gaviria liberalized

economic policies in what was called "*la apertura*," opening the door for foreign investment by instituting reduced tariffs, privatizing state-owned businesses, and adopting a more liberal foreign exchange rate, among other things.

Under the Uribe administration, as noted above, increased security has benefited the economy. Both gross national product and foreign investment have increased under his watch, while inflation has remained low. Today, Colombia is luring foreign investment with vast untapped oil and mineral stores and twenty-year ironclad contractual guarantees.

Colombia is a service economy, with more than 50 percent of the gross domestic product coming from the service sector. The main industries are petroleum and mining, especially coal and gold. Its main agricultural exports are coffee and cut flowers, followed by bananas and tropical fruits, and many others.

Colombia is rich in mineral and petroleum reserves, making mining and oil big business today. It is South America's number one coal producer and the third-largest oil producer, behind Brazil and Venezuela. With the discovery of 1.5 billion barrels of petroleum in the Cusiana and Cupiagua fields, analysts predict that Colombia will overtake Venezuelan oil production within ten years. Gold is still mined, as well as silver, nickel, platinum, lead, and Colombia's world-famous emeralds.

It is hard to measure Colombia's illegal exports, but the exposure of money-laundering schemes to hide billions of US dollars coming into the Colombian economy indicate that vast illegal narcotics revenues continue to come in. Colombia's largest trade partners have traditionally been the USA and Venezuela; currently the country is pursuing free trade agreements with the USA, Europe, Asia, and Canada to open markets further. Colombia is a member of the Andean Community of Nations, one of two South American trade blocs, in partnership with Bolivia, Ecuador, and Peru. The Andean Community of Nations merged with South America's largest trade bloc, Mercosur, which, in 2008, formed the Union of South American

Nations (UNASUR), with the intention of modeling a South American Free Trade Area after the European Union.

Increased Security and International Investment
President Uribe focused on developing and expanding international trade markets. Foreign investment is allowed in all sectors of the economy except in national security and the disposal of hazardous waste. Most of Colombia's industries are now privatized, while some electrical and energy companies remain state owned. International investments are treated equally in terms of the law, both legally and administratively. The USA is currently Colombia's largest foreign investor.

International investors are increasingly attracted to the investment opportunities they are finding in Colombia. Many are attracted to its large and qualified labor force, high literacy rate, stable currency, and increased spending on infrastructure and security. More than seven hundred multinational companies have holdings there. The Colombian government continues to pass business friendly reforms that encourage foreign investment, including 100 percent ownership of financial institutions by foreign investors, increased profit remittance ceilings, a reduction in currency controls, and more flexible hiring and firing practices, all of which are making Colombia attractive to foreign investors.

Emergence from Dark Times
With increased security has come a cultural awakening. Safer streets make people feel alive again as they emerge from terrible times. Collectively, Colombians are going through a period of self-discovery, reflecting on what has happened to their country during the armed conflict, and beginning to face up to the horrible atrocities that have

taken place, while trying to redefine themselves for the future. Most Colombians have been affected by the conflict, directly or indirectly, victims of a group of criminals who have held the country in a state of siege and perpetual fear. The violence over the past years has isolated the country and the people from the rest of the world, halting tourism and limiting personal freedoms and movement within the country. Now, as the violence wanes, Colombians are starting to recover, and you can feel the freshness in the air.

Bogotanos are giddy with freedom and the city is buzzing with new life. You can gauge the commitment to the future in new openings—newspapers, art galleries, specialty retail boutiques, gourmet coffee shops, upscale restaurants, art expos, concerts in the park. People are opening themselves to investment in the future. Bogotá has become a restaurant city after years of being a place that closed up at night in fear. The inhabitants are enjoying their city again— strolling through city parks during the day and sipping cocktails on rooftop bars at night. Even as recent events continue to show that the security situation is still unpredictable, Bogotá's August 2010 terrorist bombing shook the capital but not the confidence of its residents, stock market, or foreign investors.

COLOMBIA IN THE WORLD

Colombia has the fourth-largest economy in South America behind Brazil, Venezuela, and Argentina, and the fifth largest in Latin America behind Mexico. Colombians say their country is a first-, second-, and third-world country all at the same time—highly advanced in some ways and developing in others.

Colombia sees its neighbors as siblings. In some ways they are related: they all have something in common, though some get along and some don't. Colombia and Venezuela have a love-hate relationship. They were once family, united as one country in Bólivar's Gran Colombia. They share similar geography, history, and culture. As the only non-leftist government amongst their close neighbors, Colombia sees Venezuelan President Hugo Chavez as a leftist threat. Personally Colombians view upper-class Venezuelans as "nouveau riche," wealthy but tacky, low class and uncultured. Ecuador is the obnoxious younger brother. Bolivia is seen as a silly cousin who just isn't taken that seriously. Colombians find the Argentineans arrogant, even though Argentinean style and beauty are secretly admired, and Mexicans are criticized for seeing themselves as North American instead of Latin American.

Colombia's relations with Ecuador and Venezuela are strained today, largely due to border conflicts arising from cross-border operations in pursuit of insurgent groups, and to their left-leaning policies. Colombia accuses both countries of allowing FARC guerrillas to take shelter in their border regions.

In April 2010 Ecuador's leftist president Rafael Correa reissued an arrest warrant for the then Colombian Minister of Defense and now president, Juan Manuel Santos, an indicator that relations are not repaired.

Computer files recovered from a FARC camp have tied the Venezuelan government to the FARC, accusations that Venezuela's president Hugo Chavez strongly denies.

Colombia's strong ties with the USA play into disputes with the leftist governments of Venezuela and Ecuador, both characterized by varying degrees of anti-American sentiment. In response to a Colombian–USA military pact, Venezuela instituted a trade freeze against Colombia.

VALUES &
ATTITUDES

The Colombian people have been shaped by their landscape and by their complex history. Colombia's wild geography has historically made communication and travel between regions difficult, which forced people to be self-reliant and independent. And because the rugged topography made some regions hard to access, they were difficult to govern, giving rise to lawlessness.

Colombians come from agrarian roots, which makes them hardworking and motivated. From Spanish colonial rule they inherited a hierarchical class structure that still is the foundation of Colombian society. The extreme social and economic inequality that this created led to discontent and conflict, the results of which have been more than forty years of violence. Colombia's unprecedented armed conflict has affected all its citizens in some way, yet the people have come through the difficulties with great dignity. From these collective experiences they have developed a range of characteristics that sometimes seem contradictory. The Colombians are a paradox.

Colombians are refined and traditional, conservative and Catholic, guided by strict social mores that have been passed down since colonial times. Many are warm and open, friendly and fun loving; others are self-absorbed and self-important. But they are also rebels—strong individualists who take matters into their own hands and skirt the rules if necessary. They are savvy entrepreneurs, sophisticated and forward thinking in a quickly changing country. They are cosmopolitan and, at the same time, agrarian. And, no matter what, they put adversity aside for a good time: they are hard workers who party all night and still wake up for work the next day.

As we have seen, Colombia is experiencing a period of rapid modernization. The country's launch into the modern world has much to do with its recent history. The last five decades of armed conflict have hindered all aspects of Colombian life, but as the situation brightens Colombians are rushing toward the future with hope and excitement, making up for lost time. Remembering this will help a visitor recognize and interpret the complicated and often contradictory behavior of a people who are deeply traditional but feeling frisky, slowly being liberated from horrible times.

THE FAMILY

The family is at the heart of Colombian life. Family comes before work, friends and even private time. Families spend a lot of time together, much more than in the USA. Entire families have weekly meals together, go on a *paseo* (country outing) on weekends, and spend holidays and often vacations together. Colombians tend to define themselves in terms of "the group" in every aspect of their lives—in regionalism, social class, and the country club—but one's family is the first and most important group in life.

Colombian families traditionally have been large, with as many as seven to ten children. When social life revolves around a family that size, obligations can be overwhelming and keep everyone busy: weekly family dinners, weekends out of town at the family *finca* (country house or farm), as well as important events like weddings, baptisms, first communions, birthdays, and *quinceañeras* (fifteenth birthdays), and of course all the holidays.

¡Qué Mono!

People love babies in all countries, but in Colombia their fascination stands out. Walking down a Bogotá street with your baby, you will get a smile from every single person walking by, something unusual in the city, where people to do not greet each other in passing. Babies are welcome in fine dining restaurants, where waiters will go out of their way to make sure your baby is happy.

Don't be alarmed if someone calls a fair-skinned baby "*mono.*" They are not calling your baby a monkey! It means "lovely" in Spanish, and in Colombia it also means "white" or "fair." If a baby has a fair complexion, you will hear "*Qué mono,*" the highest compliment, referring to the baby's "whiteness"—light skin, blond hair, or blue eyes— all attributes that are highly valued in Colombian society.

Children usually live at home with their parents until they marry. When they do venture out to live on their own, they are expected to come back to spend holidays. It is not uncommon to see thirty- or even forty-year-old "kids" with careers and lives of their own still living with their parents. A Colombian friend confessed that she felt so guilty about wanting to spend Christmas with friends instead of family that it took her seven years to muster up the courage to tell her mother.

Now urban families are having fewer children, more like two to four. But even with smaller families the importance of a big family circle is still alive. In Colombia they say that "if there is food for one, there is food for two," so additions to family gatherings are welcome. The elders are the glue that holds families together and are always included. The circle grows even bigger with non-blood relatives, close friends, and *padrinos* (godparents), who also play an active role in family life.

Men's Roles and *Machismo*

Men have traditionally been the head of the Colombian family, earning the money and making the decisions. Although young men are changing their attitudes somewhat, men rarely help out with domestic duties. They do not take active roles in caring for children, do not take their kids to the park without their wives, and they do not change diapers. While women's roles expand as they enter the workforce, they continue to be responsible for taking care of the children and the house when their workday is done.

Although not as evident as in other countries in Latin America, *machismo* exists in Colombia in varying degrees depending on social class. Within upper-class circles one doesn't feel *machismo* much anymore but throughout middle- and lower-class circles it is more prevalent. Society still permits men to behave in ways women cannot, even as women have taken a stronger role in society.

In all social classes it remains more acceptable for a man to stray outside the marriage, while women are expected to remain faithful. Married men frequently keep a *querida* (lover) on the side. Often the wife will be aware of her rival but tolerate this behavior for many years. Yet many

Colombian women are tired of the double standard and are changing their ways. In Bogotá, "modern" women are saying that if married men cheat, then they will too.

In Colombia's more conservative areas, like Bogotá, the practice of keeping a lover is not publicly accepted, so one is expected to be discreet. On the Caribbean coast, where Caribbean culture conforms to its own standards, many men make it a matter of pride to keep lovers openly all over town.

In regions of the country strongly affected by the ongoing armed conflict *machismo* is strong. The accepted level of violence and lawlessness bleeds into male/female relations. In these areas violence and rape are widespread, and infidelity and early pregnancy are common.

Women's Roles
Historically upper-class women were not permitted to work outside the house and were expected to stay home in charge of domestic matters. The situation has been somewhat different in middle- and lower-class families, where, out of necessity, both parents have to work to make ends meet. In rural areas where poverty is high or families have been displaced by the armed conflict, men often are financially forced to seek work away from the home, leaving the women as the de facto heads of the household.

Today traditional roles for men and women change as society changes. Strong, educated women have entered the workforce with great success. Over the last five years women have flooded the business world, now leading companies as top executives and running for president. Colombia has more women in politics and higher elected office than almost anywhere in Latin America. Working women contribute financially to the family, giving them more power and say in family matters. Today decision making is more often shared between the man and women due to their shared economic power within the relationship.

SOCIAL CLASS AND STATUS

Although Colombia's population is ethnically diverse, Colombian society is highly stratified. Your position in society is determined by your ancestry, family name, the color of your skin, and finally your income. Social mobility is difficult. Since Spanish rule, those with pure European blood, "whites," have held the highest positions in society, controlling the government, owning most of the land, and dominating trade and commerce. Today, the wealthy elite—still of European descent—constitutes a small portion of the population but continues to hold all the power. The sons and daughters of former presidents are important figures who run for office to keep political power within the family, in what one journalist has called the "power dynasties."

The rich upper class sticks together in a sort of elite social club in which rules of entry are strict, and outsiders are not easily welcomed. Wealth alone is not enough to buy you entry. In Bogotá the rich live and play in a self-contained bubble in the northern part of the city, separate from the rest of society. Rarely do upper-class people venture into the southern sector of the city.

Neighborhoods in Bogotá, Medellín, and Cali are divided into official *estratos*, socioeconomic strata in which neighborhood is classified by social class. The cities' poorest live in *estrato 1*, and the wealthiest in *estrato 6*. For a Bogotano the *estrato* they live in is a determining factor in many things, indicating clearly one's place in society. Many Bogotanos will make great sacrifices to move up into a higher *estrato*, knowing that extreme value is placed on outward appearances.

Los Magicos

The upper classes, apart from being wealthy, adhere to certain moral values and social mores. Entry into the upper classes requires one to come from "cultured" ancestry with a "good" family name. But with the rise of the illegal drug trade in the 1980s, an emerging class of the superwealthy appeared in high society circles and took the elites by surprise. In a society where the social thoroughbreds are a tight-knit group who all know each other, these newcomers were complete strangers who appeared overnight, buying houses in the most exclusive neighborhoods of Bogotá and Medellín. To high society they seemed to have gotten rich overnight, as if by magic. *Los magicos* were shunned in elite circles, considered *mal educado* (uneducated, uncultured, and rude.) Even with tons of new money, the narco-millionaires could not buy admittance to the club. Quietly called *los lobos* (the wolves), they are seen as individuals—very, very rich ones—of undistinguished ancestral backgrounds and questionable values, unfit for elevated social circles.

RELIGION

The Roman Catholic Church in Colombia is considered one of the most conservative in Latin America, and has been a powerful force in the country's history. Since Spanish colonial rule, Colombia has been a staunchly conservative Catholic country, with as much as 90 percent of the population Roman Catholic. The Church has been the overriding influence in politics, education, and family life, closely allying itself with the Conservative party. During the politically charged period of La Violencia, the Church supported the Conservatives in their slaughter of Liberals. Some priests publicly condoned the killing of Liberals in the name of the Church.

The Church's power remains evident in Colombian society today. Abortion is still illegal, except to protect the health of the mother in case of emergency and in cases of rape. Divorce is illegal following a Catholic Church wedding, and civil weddings were made legal only in 1973.

Up until 1991 the Roman Catholic Church was the official state Church of Colombia.

Although most Colombians consider themselves Roman Catholic, some are more religious than others. In rural areas both men and women are deeply devout, attending church regularly every Sunday or more. They celebrate holidays with town *fiestas*, elaborate religious processions, and deeply personal devotions.

Urban populations in all socioeconomic classes tend to be more lax regarding their regular Sunday mass attendance, but the majority still consider themselves Catholics. Most go to church during the weeks of Easter (Semana Santa), Christmas, and for weddings, baptisms, and first communions—but not much more often, an indicator that urban Colombians might not be as pious as they once were.

THE BODY BEAUTIFUL

Colombians take outward appearances seriously. How you look signals your position in society. Physical features play a big role. The wealthy make every attempt to look "good," which to them means light skinned, tall, slim, and with curves. Colombians value a curvy figure and a well-sculpted body.

In Colombia urbanites are sporty and active. They are in shape. Few upper- or middle-class Colombians are fat. Many do some sort of physical activity regularly, including jogging, cycling, yoga, aerobics, or going to the gym.

Unlike in some Latin American countries, in big cities there is a rising consciousness about health foods, low fat diets, and organic foods and farming. This means you can buy your chicken hormone free, *pollo criollo*, and your vegetables grown organically—using clean water and without pesticides.

Boob Jobs, Botox, and Beauty Pageants

Colombians want a sculpted body, and when the gym isn't paying off, cosmetic surgery is an available and accepted option. This is not as expensive in Colombia as it is in the USA and Europe, and it is in high demand, so plastic surgeons are doing good business. Popular procedures include eye lifts, face-lifts, nose jobs, liposuction, tummy tucks, breast implants, even bottom implants for a curvier look. Some parents even give their young daughter cosmetic surgery as a gift on her fifteenth birthday, sometimes a nose job or breast implants. Cosmetic surgery is so popular that tourists are coming to Colombia searching out cheap procedures in what is called "cosmetic tourism."

Beauty pageants run all year-long in small towns all over Colombia, determining contestants for the revered Miss Colombia pageant held in Cartagena every November. The entire country stops to watch the Miss Colombia pageant, all eyes glued to their television sets. Television networks give top coverage to the pageant with critics examining every feature of every contestant, every fake eyelash, artificial implant, and ripple of cellulite. Cosmetic surgery is an accepted means of improving your natural attributes.

On Colombian streets you will see adults as well as teenagers from all socioeconomic backgrounds with braces on their teeth. Colombia is one of the most affordable places in South America to have dental work done. Maids, nannies, doormen, taxi drivers, even flower vendors on the street have them.

JOIE DE VIVRE

Colombians say that any excuse is a good excuse for a party, and have a *fiesta* spirit, a joy for life, in spite of hard times. They love to entertain, party, dance, and enjoy themselves, no matter their class, race, or economic status. They show a genuine love for their culture, their unique regional music, and their country. Costeños (people from the coast) are famous for their wild boisterous side and zest for merrymaking, exemplified in their annual party—Carnaval. But you are sure to find the rest of Colombia in party mode too.

There are all-night parties any night of the week. There are Wednesday night parties that actually start at 9:00 p.m., or 3:00 a.m., a continuation at home after the bars close. There are midnight mariachis (Mexican traditional big band ensembles featuring violins, guitars, trumpets, and forceful vocals), during which the bands serenade young lovers, celebrate birthdays, and offer apologies after lovers' quarrels. December is the month of never-ending parties in certain neighborhoods.

In urban apartment living, everyone in the neighborhood gets the party experience, even if they are not invited. Colombians have a much higher tolerance level for the noise of neighborhood festivities and rarely complain or call the police. Colombians say: if the noise bothers you, just join in. Foreigners are often stunned by this —a complete disregard for their neighbors. All-night parties next door while you are trying to sleep can be extremely frustrating, especially because no one else seems to mind it except you! It is just part of the culture. So, a good pair of earplugs in your luggage will probably come in handy.

ATTITUDES TO THE LAW: ANY MEANS NECESSARY

Colombians love outlaws—rebels who by "any means necessary" employ their own private justice to fight against an unjust society. Pablo Escobar was lovingly called "the Paisa Robin Hood." Historically in certain areas of the country people have been accustomed to taking matters into their own hands to get things done, inspiring a culture of vigilantism and corruption instead of a culture of law.

For the narco-kingpins "getting things done" means bribing local officials, judges, customs agents, police, and anyone else they can pay to look the other way. In the department of Antioquia a culture of *contrabandistas* and organized crime already existed and easily set the stage for the cocaine traffickers in the 1980s. Throughout the armed conflict, private citizens have formed paramilitary groups to fight the guerrillas and protect their interests when the government did not. Although Colombians are rule followers when it comes to obeying cumbersome bureaucratic processes, the rule of law has traditionally been weak in Colombia, making it easy for outlaws to win and corruption to flourish. When it comes to the rules of the road, anything goes.

Throughout Colombian history power has remained in the hands of very few, leaving many to fend for themselves. With social mobility almost impossible, Colombians celebrate the outcast figure championing the common man's triumph over the social elite.

CLASS AND RACE

In Colombian society, people are judged by their class above all else, and attitudes about race come into play. For example, "white" peasants and servants of European descent are common, but you will rarely see an Afro-Colombian among the upper classes. Many Colombians say there is no racism in the country since everyone is of mixed race, pointing out that their society is "classist," not racist. Yet, even though social class determines one's place in society over race, a dark skin and indigenous traits are considered negatives, while light skin, hair, and eyes are admired. Colombians prefer to point out their European heritage. Light skin and pure European descent are highly valued, an idea instilled by the Spanish in colonial times. While marrying outside one's class is now more accepted than in the past, the upper class still tend to marry within

their circle, keeping European bloodlines pure. Although not seen today, the desire to guard European bloodlines meant that, in the past, marrying within the family was not uncommon.

Before mass urbanization, Colombians of different races lived in separate parts of the country and had little contact with each other. Only now, since a variety of races are living in close proximity, is race a topic of discussion.

Class hierarchies and racial inequality are so ingrained in Colombia's social structure that they are seen as the normal order of things.

Colombia's large Afro-Colombian population is descended from African slaves brought by the Spanish to

Cartagena to work in the gold mines along the Caribbean coast. Peter Wade, a British social anthropologist, has observed that the Afro-Colombian's self-image reveals their feelings about race in their society. He observed that racial intermarriage, common in Afro-Colombian populations, occurs as a way of "marrying up" racially, what is termed *blanqueamiento*—the process of bleaching away one's blackness to help one's offspring move up in society by being less black.

ATTITUDES TOWARD FOREIGNERS

Colombians will tell you they love foreigners and will talk to anybody, but of course it depends. The upper classes respect well turned out people like themselves, *"gente de bien."* If you don't pass the test you might feel snubbed. In the country, people are more open and friendly and eager to talk to you.

Bogotanos are big city people who tend to keep to themselves if they don't know you. Foreigners sometimes describe Bogotanos as cool and distant. But don't get bothered by it. Once you give someone a warm *"buenos días,"* you will get a warm smile in return. To really be accepted into Colombian circles you need a social introduction. With this entrée you will be well received.

DIGNITY AND NATIONAL PRIDE

Most Colombians are proud of their country and are deeply ashamed of the conflict and violence that has overcome it. Most are disgusted with the drug trafficking world, and are upstanding citizens who are appalled by the atrocities that have taken place in their own country. In the face of adversity, they have managed to maintain their dignity.

Colombians are extremely concerned with their international image and want to set the record straight.

They will jump at the opportunity to tell foreigners that their streets are not teeming with armed gunmen and drug traffickers. They want you to understand that there is more to Colombia than what you have heard in the news. Moreover, Colombians want the world to know about their country's spectacular untouched beauty and biodiversity, their vibrant cosmopolitan culture, their world-class cities, and their rich literary and artistic history—which don't usually come to mind when you think of Colombia.

STRONG WORK ETHIC

Despite the country's great natural wealth, most Colombians are not rich and have always had to undertake strenuous work. They are, in general, hardworking and industrious. Over all, they take business dealings seriously, show up more or less on time, and follow through. Yet, people who you might employ to do a service do not like to tell you "no," and as a result there could be some misunderstandings about when, exactly, the work will be done.

TIMEKEEPING

Colombians live on two different times depending on the occasion. People show up for official business—business meetings, doctor's appointments, airplane schedules, opera and theater—on time. But for social and more casual engagements they live on *"tiempo colombiano"* (Colombian time), which means late to very late. Be prepared to wait, and bring a book to occupy the time because Colombian time can run anywhere from an hour to two hours late (see page 86).

chapter three

CUSTOMS & TRADITIONS

Today Colombia's customs and traditions are mostly based upon those brought by the Spanish in the sixteenth century. Unlike some Latin American countries whose traditions are a synthesis of indigenous and Spanish rituals, in most areas of Colombia, with a few exceptions, the folk tradition reflects European roots. Overall, very little of Colombia's indigenous culture is accessible to the general population and most urban Colombians don't know much about their pre-Hispanic past. Without searching them out, a visitor won't get a feel for Colombia's indigenous traditions.

The Colombian calendar is full of days off work, a combination of both religious and national holidays. Urban residents celebrate their days off in a low key way with family and friends, without fireworks, street fairs, or a big to-do. Northern Bogotá is a ghost town on *puente* (bridge, or long) weekends, when most people leave the city and head to their country house (or *finca*), to spend their weekend relaxing. Rural villages celebrate Catholic holidays with more fanfare, ornate processions, and a town *fiesta* (party or celebration).

Colombia's Caribbean coast is the exception. When the Spanish brought African slaves to Colombia during the colonial period, those slaves brought their native traditions with them. Today Colombia's Afro-Colombian culture is a rich blend of African and inherited Spanish Catholic customs, mixed with what remains of indigenous Colombian traditions. This *mestizaje*, or mixture, comes through in everything Afro-Colombian—in the food, the music and dance, and their famous Carnaval.

FESTIVALS AND HOLIDAYS

There are so many public holidays in Colombia that it seems like every Monday is a day off work. Many of these are regarded today as simply days of rest rather than specific religious holidays. Today Colombians mainly celebrate the Immaculate Conception or Día de Las Velitas, Christmas, Carnaval, Easter Week (Semana Santa), Independence Day, and have imported Halloween.

What Holiday Is It Today, Anyway?

I still can't keep track of what holidays there are in Colombia, there are so many. But, apparently I am not alone. Walking down the street in Bogotá one holiday Monday, I asked a Colombian who was walking beside me, "So, what holiday are we celebrating today, anyway?" He replied with a smile, "Oh, who knows, some saint's birthday."

Día de Las Velitas (Day of the Candles: December 7–8)

Día de Las Velitas is the Colombian celebration of the feast of the Immaculate Conception and is the unofficial start of the Christmas season. On the night of December 7 Colombians join in processions through town carrying candlelit paper lanterns, then, in honor of the Virgin, place their glowing lanterns in their windows when they get home; or, people carry luminous paper lanterns to neighborhood parks, where they are left to light up the night.

In the Spanish colonial town of Villa de Leyva in the department of Boyacá, on December 7 and 8 they celebrate the Día de Las Velitas in what this town calls the Festival de las Luces (Festival of Lights). On the eve of December 7, town residents place flickering candles on their balconies and terraces and use them to line the streets, and put on an extravagant fireworks show in the town square.

Navidad (Christmas: December 24–25)

During the Christmas season, Medellín and Bogotá hang up thousands of *alumbrados navideños* (Christmas illuminations), setting up enormous light sculpture displays in many city parks and bathing the urban areas in a bright glow. Apartment dwellers light up their balconies and windows with multicolored flashing, running, and twinkling lights that sparkle in a nervous flutter. Throughout the season families stroll through the parks

to enjoy the nightly light shows. News anchors do evening reports on which neighborhood parks have the most, the best, or the brightest light displays. Bogotá's main plaza,

Plaza Bolivar, is filled with rows of shiny red tinsel trees surrounding a giant green Christmas tree decorated with bright yellow sunflowers.

Colombians celebrate Christmas Eve at home with family. Christmas foods differ by region. In the interior in and around Bogotá a traditional Christmas Eve dinner is roasted turkey, *tamales* (steamed dough with meat or cheese), *ajiaco santafereño* (chicken and potato stew from Bogotá,), and *buñuelos* (round doughnuts with cheese.) Everyone stays until midnight to open gifts and wish each other an emotional Merry Christmas with hugs all around. Some families attend Midnight Mass *(misa de media noche)* but not all.

On Christmas Day families traditionally go for out for lunch to an *asadero*, an open-air barbeque restaurant in the country that serves typical grilled meats, sausage, potatoes, corn, *yuca* (cassava), and desserts. They relax and recover from the festivities of the night before. Families stay at home in the evening and eat the Christmas Eve leftovers.

Adults exchange gifts at midnight on Christmas Eve, but children younger than eight years old find their presents next to their beds on Christmas Day when they wake up. Colombians put up a Nativity Scene (El Pesebre), and decorate Christmas trees, hang stockings from the mantels, and have adopted Santa Claus into their tradition. Traditionally El Niño Dios (the Christ Child) brings gifts to the children, but nowadays gifts may come from Papa Noel or Santa Claus as well.

Bogotá is quiet in December. Kids are out of school for over a month so anyone who can takes a long vacation. Traffic eases and city streets become manageable. Bogotá closes down from December 24 through 25 and on New Year's Eve through the weekend. Restaurants, grocery stores, banks, and shops are shut tight.

Año Nuevo (New Year's Eve: December 31 and New Year's Day: January 1)

New Year's Eve is celebrated with a big gathering involving family and friends, dinner, cocktails, and much revelry. The New Year's dinner is similar to Christmas Eve. Everyone counts down the seconds until midnight, when everyone hugs and kisses and yells *"Feliz Año,"* "Happy New Year." Then the party goes on until morning.

Some Colombians follow special traditions to ensure luck and prosperity in the New Year. Like the Italians, some make sure the dinner table is laden with fruit, making sure to eat twelve grapes, one for each month. Others put a handful of dried beans or lentils in each corner of the house. Yet others fill a suitcase with clothes and leave it at the front door of the house overnight, hoping for a New Year filled with travel.

Semana Santa (Holy Week)

Semana Santa, also known as Semana Mayor, is Colombia's most holy holiday. Special masses are attended on Jueves

Santo (Holy Thursday), Viernes Santo (Good Friday), and Domingo de Resurrección (Easter Sunday.) Holy Week is celebrated throughout Colombia with passion plays on Jueves Santo and somber processions on Viernes Santo, including re-creations of the Stations of the Cross and the Crucifixion.

Popayán's solemn Semana Santa processions, a sixteenth-century tradition that continues today, are the most elaborate in Colombia. Winding through the streets of Popayán on a route in the shape of the Cross, barefoot men, the *cargueros,* carry enormous carved wooden structures on their shoulders honoring the life and death of Jesus Christ. The processions weave through the cobblestone streets of the Spanish colonial town for hours.

On the night of Jueves Santo, in the small mountain town of Monguí, townspeople follow the passion play through town. They make their way up narrow cobblestone streets to the top of the town where an eerie human silhouette of the Crucifixion is projected down to the congregation below. Also worth seeing are the famous Good Friday processions in Tunja, Boyacá, that culminate in the Plaza Principal.

Independence Day (July 20)
Colombians celebrate their Independence from Spain, declared on July 20, 1810, with military parades in major cities. Many people enjoy the day off by going out of town if the calendar allows for a *puente,* a long holiday weekend with Friday or Monday off work.

Carnaval (four days before Lent)
Barranquilla's Carnaval is Colombia's biggest and most culturally interesting party, in which indigenous Colombian, African, and European traditions have fused to create a unique creative expression. Starting four days before Lent, Colombians show their wild side with days of

all-day, all-night merrymaking. Colombia's Carnaval won recognition as a "Masterpiece of Oral and Intangible Heritage of Humanity" by UNESCO in 2008. Colombians are proud of their rich tradition, considered second only to that of Brazil.

In the sixteenth century, the Spanish *conquistadores* established one of their first cities in Barranquilla on Colombia's Caribbean coast. Inevitably their cultural traditions mixed with those of the indigenous Colombians

and the Africans they soon brought as slaves. Today's Carnaval blends all of these cultural traditions, visible in every aspect of the party. Elaborately costumed and masked dancers showing lots of skin groove to the Afro-Caribbean beats of the cumbia, and variant styles of the puya and porro. Carnaval dances mix the traditional African congo with the European paloteo and the indigenous mico mica. African, European, and Indigenous sounds merge using a variety of percussion and wind folk instruments—*gaitas, maracas, claves, congas, güiras,* and *timbales.* Streets fill with wildly decorated floats and thousands of revelers. Pasto, in the southern department of Nariño, is also known for its *carnaval,* the Festival de Blancos y Negros (Festival of the Whites and Blacks.)

Festival de las Flores (Flower Festival: July 28–August 7)

Medellín's annual Festival de las Flores is a celebration of regional pride. Every year the streets overflow with millions of flowers in celebration of Antioquias's constant springlike climate and long flower-growing tradition. The highlight is the Desfile de los Silleteros that takes place in the first week of August, a local tradition since 1957. Farming families from the Santa Elena neighborhood make elaborate and enormous flower arrangements mounted on wooden structures that they carry on their backs during the parade. Being a *silletero* is a matter of local pride in Santa Elena, where they have passed down the tradition now through four generations. Days before the parade you can watch the *silleteros* (named for the giant chairlike structure on which the arrangements are created) designing their masterpieces.

SAINT'S DAYS AND PILGRIMAGES

Many Colombians have a favorite saint, of which they carry a picture and prayer card with them. They wear a cross and bless themselves for good luck. Only small rural towns celebrate saint's days in earnest, with mass and town fiestas, saint's days are considered national days off and no one complains. Colombians are definitely devoted believers. There are sightings of manifestations of the Virgin Mary all the time, including a weeping Virgen de Rosario statue in Pasto, and images of the Virgin etched into staple foods such as the skin of a mango and the surface of an *arepa* (corn flat bread). The Cult of Mary is strong throughout the country. The most pious make pilgrimages to show their devotion to the Virgin or to El Divino Niño (the Divine Child). Devotees of the Virgin flock to the miraculously restored sixteenth-century painting of her in the town of Chiquinquirá in the department of Boyacá. Every Sunday in Bogotá more than

100,000 believers make a pilgrimage to El Sanctuario del Divino Niño Jesus to pray for miracles.

Nuestra Señora de Chiquinquirá (July 9)
The Virgin of Chiquinquirá is Colombia's patron saint. In the sixteenth century, the Spanish painter Alonso de Narváez painted the *Virgin of the Rosary*, using natural pigments made from herbs, plants, and the earth of the region. As his canvas, he used a piece of cotton fabric made by the local indigenous people. In 1562, the painting of the Virgin was placed in a chapel with a leaky roof that let in the elements, and over time the cotton began to disintegrate, and the image faded to the point that it was hardly recognizable. In 1577 the damaged painting was taken to the modest chapel of Chiquinquirá, where it remained in the back room, ruined and forgotten. Eight years later, a local Spanish woman, María Ramos, decided to clean up the chapel, and hung the damaged canvas at the altar, and prayed.

On December 26, 1587, a miracle happened—the image on the canvas was instantaneously restored to its original glory, as bright and clear and beautiful as before. Today, believers continue to make pilgrimages to pray to her miraculous image.

FOLKLORE AND SUPERSTITIONS
Rural communities still incorporate vestiges of pre-Hispanic or African traditions into their daily lives, including shamanism. They might be Catholic and pray to their favorite saint but they might also employ non-Christian remedies for their physical and spiritual needs. Both urban and rural *plazas del mercados* (market squares) have stalls selling medicinal plants and herbal remedies.

Many believe in the power of good and bad spells and use traditional healers who practice indigenous rituals to cleanse a person of bad spirits or evil spells. Remote jungle tribes like the Emberas in Chocó and many Amazonian tribes incorporate magic and ritual into their everyday lives, and rely heavily on shamans as medicine men, healers, and priests. The shaman administers medicinal plant potions and summons the spirit world through hallucinogenic drinks to rid the patient of evil spirits and illness. In major cities tarot readings are popular. In Bogotá stores along one of the main thoroughfares, Avenida Caracas, cater to the needs of the traditional healer—herbs, potions, incense, and "good luck baths."

Thirsty Spirits

Some believe that when a person dies that their spirit returns to their house before it moves to the next dimension. The spirits get very thirsty and need water to help them pass smoothly into the spirit world. When someone dies, glasses of water are placed all over the house so the spirit can drink its fill before moving on.

TRADITIONAL MUSIC AND DANCE
Vallenato

Vallenato is Colombia's folk music and is popular throughout the country. Its sound is a synthesis of Colombian cultural traditions—Spanish mixed with African and indigenous Amerindian. Vallenato is a uniquely Colombian sound. It inspires a lot of arm waving and knee tapping and guarantees a good time. The songs have contagious melodies with upswing beats, so don't be surprised if you leave Colombia humming vallenato long after you get home. Even city slickers who claim to not like it secretly do.

Vallenato has fusion roots originating along the Caribbean coast around Valledupar in the northern department of César. Its singsong sound is traditionally played with three instruments: a German accordion, an African *caja* drum, and a *guacharaca*, an indigenous rhythm instrument. The all male big band, complete with an array of percussion instruments and back-up singers, are guided by a charismatic lead singer who can hit the high notes. Valledupar celebrates its native music with its annual Festival de La Leyenda Vallenata at the end of April.

Cumbia

Cumbia is the sultry tropical rhythm of the Colombian Caribbean and the soundtrack of Carnaval, characterized

by its heavy African drumbeat, a tiny horn section, *gaitas* (indigenous flutes), the slow roll of *maracas*, and elements of Spanish music. The cumbia is a musical *mestizaje* (mélange), a musical history of this diversely populated coast, in which the cultures collide to create something altogether new.

The dance is sensuous and seductive, movements inherited from native African dance traditions, with tight twisting footwork said to represent slaves' feet shuffling in chains. Girls traditionally wear flowers in their hair, off-the-shoulder long sleeved blouses and long flowing Spanish skirts that twirl with the turn of the feet and the swing of the hips. Men wear white pants and shirts with red handkerchiefs tied around their necks.

Salsa

Salsa might be native to Puerto Rico and Cuba but Colombians have made the tropical sound and swinging moves their own. The capital of Colombian salsa is Cali, in the department of Cauca, where the best salsa bands and sexiest dancers strut their stuff at Cali's annual Festival de Salsa in July and at the Feria de Cali every December.

Bogotá is not known to be a salsa center, but salsa fills the airwaves on local radio stations and can be heard nightly pouring out of *salsatecas*. Some of the best salsa dancers come out of Cali, Colombia—so even if a Colombian says they don't salsa, you can assume that really they know how. So a few lessons before you arrive (as salsa lessons are hard to come by in Bogotá) would be a good idea if you want to keep up on the dance floor.

Mariachi

Of course, mariachi is not native to Colombia, but Colombians have taken to the Mexican crooners, who are well represented in many major cities. Mariachi bands are known for the *serenata* and have cornered this niche market in Colombia. Men often hire a mariachi group to serenade a lover, right at midnight, considered the hour of romance. Sometimes the *serenata* is a declaration of love or a birthday wish, other times it's a pleading for forgiveness. Either way, trumpets announce the mariachi band's nocturnal arrival. No matter how beautiful the music, if the *serenata* is not for you and you have to work the next day, you might not feel that romantic. Make sure to have your earplugs handy.

THE FESTIVAL CALENDAR
RELIGIOUS AND NATIONAL HOLIDAYS

* If they do not fall on a Monday, these holidays are celebrated on the following Monday, making for a long weekend.

January 1 Año Nuevo (New Year's Day)

January 6 Día de los Reyes Magos (Three Kings' Day—Epiphany)*

March 19 Día de San Jose (Saint Joseph's Day)*

March/April Semana Santa (Holy Week)

Jueves Santo (Holy Thursday)

Viernes Santo (Holy Friday)

Domingo de Resurrección (Easter Sunday)

May 1 Primero de Mayo—Día del Trabajo (First of May—Labor Day)

May 20 La Ascensión del Señor (Ascension of Christ)*

June 10 Corpus Christi*

June 18 Sagrado Corazón (Sacred Heart)*

June 29 Día de San Pedro y San Pablo (Saint Peter's and Saint Paul's Day)*

July 20 Día de la Independencia (Independence Day)

August 7 Batalla de Boyacá (Battle of Boyacá)

August 15 La Asunción de Nuestra Señora (Assumption of the Virgin)*

October 12 Día de la Raza (Columbus Day)*

November 1 Todos los Santos (All Saints' Day)*

November 11 Independencia de Cartagena (Independence of Cartagena)

December 8 La Inmaculada Concepción (Immaculate Conception)

December 25 Navidad (Christmas)

OTHER FESTIVALS

January 4–6 Festival de Blancos y Negros (Festival of the Whites and Blacks), Pasto

January (every two years) 2011, 2013, 2015... Festival del Diablo (Festival of the Devil), Riosucio

2nd week in January Feria de Manizales

4 days before Lent Carnaval de Barranquilla

April (every two years) 2010, 2012, 2014... Festival Iberooamericano del Teatro (Ibero-American Theater Festival), Bogotá

April (dates vary) Festival de La Leyenda Vallenata (Festival of the Vallenato Legend), Valledupar, César

July (dates vary) Festival de Salsa, Cali

July 28–August 7 Festival de Las Flores (Festival of the Flowers), Medellín

November 11 Concurso Nacional de Belleza de Colombia (Miss Colombia National Beauty Contest)

December 25–January 11 Feria de Cali

A Traditional Comeback

Good news for the *ruana*, the traditional Andean wool cloak of the Muiscas. More and more Colombians are sporting the traditional *ruana* made in Nobsa, Cundinamarca, where about 300 families carry on the weaving tradition of their ancestors. Thanks to the creative marketing skills of their mayor, on the third Sunday in May Nobsa now celebrates the *ruana* on the Internacional Dia de la Ruana (International Ruana Day).

But remember, don't call it a poncho because this makes people mad! Ponchos are from Ecuador, and serapes are from Mexico. In Colombia, it's called a *ruana*, period.

chapter four

MAKING FRIENDS

Colombians surround themselves with friends and family, and love to entertain and throw parties. Their circles are tight and their friendships strong, but if you follow a few simple rules you will have no problem making friends with them. They are warm, friendly, and outgoing once they get to know you—it might just take a while.

In turbulent times Colombians relied on family and friends for support, even protection. Colombian friendships demand total loyalty, solidarity, and discretion. Friendships usually begin when people are young, generally in school, and last for a lifetime. They build enduring friendships that survive over many miles in difficult circumstances.

In high elevations and cooler climates like Bogotá and Boyacá, individuals are reserved and may not reach out to you initially. Where the weather is warmer people tend to be more open and relaxed. In Cartagena, just a short chat might get you invited to a party that night. Rural Colombians seem fascinated with foreigners, perhaps surprised to have tourists after years of no tourism and isolation due to the armed conflict. Years of trouble gave Colombia a negative international image, deterring visitors. Therefore, given the opportunity people will want tell you their story, and to know yours. As we have seen, Colombians feel a deep sense of national pride; they love their country and want to share

it with you. If you take an interest and speak a little
Spanish, they will open up.

It Takes Time
"Mas vale viejo conocido que nuevo por conocer."

This Colombian saying reflects how long-term friendship
is valued. It means that old friends are more valuable and
more important than new ones. So, remember that it
may take some time to make friends with Colombians,
but once you do you will have friends for life.

THE FIRST CONTACT
Bogotanos will be kind and proper, but might not be
outgoing. They will take a while to gauge you—to see
if you are "cultured." This doesn't indicate they are
unfriendly. But this reserve means you will have to
make the first effort, behave properly, and give them
time. In warmer parts of the country, people tend to be
friendlier and more sociable. Greetings and small talk
are essential to all interactions, so take your time and
ease into the conversation. If you rush this part you
will be seen as rude.

Colombian society functions on social connections. Social circles are small—everyone knows each other, so you will need an introduction into a group in order to meet people. In fact, once you are introduced, Colombians will go out of their way to make you feel welcome.

If you are working in an office, your first social engagements will be going out to lunch with colleagues or for *un tinto* (a coffee) after work. Colombians are very social, group-oriented people. You will be invited to parties early on—guests think nothing of bringing extras along. You might even be invited to spend the weekend at someone's *finca* after just meeting them. Of course you should go! This is the best way to see how Colombians live.

MEETING COLOMBIANS

For long-term visitors, there are several ways in which you can get to know Colombians.

Expatriate Associations

Many expats join associations to make business and social connections, essential in Colombian society. Your embassy can provide a list of local groups. The American Society of Bogotá is a useful source for making local business connections. For women, the American Women's Club of Bogotá will help you meet both Colombians and Americans, as it includes Colombian nationals as members.

Sports and Country Clubs

As we have seen, Colombians like being part of a group so many join private clubs. Meeting people is easier if you join a club or gym because it means you have already been admitted into the group. Middle- and upper-class Colombians work out at the gym and play tennis and golf. So, sports clubs, gyms, and country clubs are possible choices and some offer shared, short-term memberships. Bogotá's aquatics center, Complejo Acuatico Simon Bolivar, is world class and offers morning and evening "open swim" times and swim groups complete with coaches, for affordable prices. Bodytech, a popular chain of upscale gyms with locations across Colombia, offers special company and embassy memberships.

Many upper-class Colombians belong to country clubs (recreational sports and social clubs) that offer swimming pools, spas, horseback riding, squash, tennis, golf, and restaurants. Golf lessons and green fees are less expensive than in the USA, making Colombia a good place to learn to play

Neighbors

Bogotá's upper-class northern neighborhoods started to spring up in the 1960s, after La Violencia riots had burned much of Bogotá to the ground, and through the 1980s and 1990s—the brutal years inflicted on Bogotanos by narco-traffickers and the armed conflict—with construction still continuing today. In Bogotá and Medellín (Colombia's drug-trading center), wealthy neighborhoods were built for protection. Since then, upper-class Colombians have lived in luxurious, yet heavily protected, high-rise apartments. Entry and exit is tightly controlled by the *portero* (doorman), who acts as control center for the building and doubles as private security. In some buildings the *portero* has to give you access to your own apartment, via an elevator that opens into your living room. It is disconcerting that, in this case, the *only* person to have a key to your apartment is the doorman!

Interaction with neighbors is minimal by design. If you do have an apartment building with a shared elevator, neighbors will exchange compulsory greetings, but issues between neighbors are handled by the *portero* and the building administrator, so there is very little contact.

WHAT SHOULD I TALK ABOUT?

If your first conversations focus on how much you like Colombia, you will be off to a good start. Ask about local foods and markets, restaurants, and "must-go" places: you will get a long list in return. Colombians believe their country is the most beautiful place on earth, so they will be happy to share their knowledge with you. They are also big fans of the arts, so discussions on film, theater, and literature are welcome.

Avoid talking about the touchier topics like politics, religion, poverty, the armed conflict, and Pablo Escobar, at least until you know people a little better. Avoid financial matters as Colombian wages differ greatly from the USA and Europe. As family is central to Colombian life, talk on this subject is welcome. Do remember your host's children's names so you can ask how they are doing the next time you see each other.

GREETINGS

All interactions in Colombia start with a formal greeting. These initial greetings are important and expected. You will use these with everyone you come in contact with— doormen, taxi drivers, receptionists, bank tellers, the corner avocado vendor, in meetings and at restaurants. If you just launch into the business at hand without the customary formalities you will be seen as uncultured and rude. You might want to practice the greetings below so you can easily roll them off your tongue.

Verbal

Conversations always start with a formal greeting depending on the time of the day—*muy buenos días* (very good morning), *buenas tardes* (good afternoon), or *buenas noches* (good evening)—see box. The concept of "afternoon" extends into what you might think of as evening, up until

7:00 or even 7:30 p.m., way after it is dark in Bogotá. Keep this in mind in the early evening, because it matters, and if you say *buenas noches* at 6:00 p.m. you will be corrected!

SOME GREETINGS
Buenos días. Cómo le ha ido? Good morning. How has it been for you?
Cómo le va? How is it going for you?
Cómo amanece? How did you rise?
Adios. Qué esté bien. Good-bye. I hope that you are well.
Adios. Qué le vaya bien. Good-bye. I hope that it goes well for you
(Use to finish your interaction.)

Following the initial greeting comes a general inquiry about one's state of being, *"Cómo le ha ido?"* ("How has it gone for you?") or the more poetic *"Cómo amanece?"* ("How did you rise?") are favored. These greetings are often followed by inquiries about one's family, their health, and the general state of things. Greetings and small talk are very important in Colombian society. They are never rushed or left out. Always spend time on the initial chitchat before moving into the second phase of conversation, because if you don't you will be perceived as rude.

For the socially complex use of the familiar form of "you" (*tú*), see pages 153–4.

Physical

The physical aspects of Colombian greetings adhere to certain traditions as well. Men greet each other with a firm handshake and an *abrazo*, a loose hug with a pat on the shoulder. Men greet women with either a handshake or one kiss on the right cheek, usually an "air kiss" in which lips never touch the cheek. Women greet other women with the "air kiss," often accompanied by an "arm clutch," which starts the same way as a handshake but the palms pass each other and clutch the forearm instead of the hand. In all cases, direct eye contact is common and expected.

THE IMPORTANCE OF TITLES

As we have seen, Colombian Spanish is full of formalities based on tradition and social hierarchy. People address each other with formal titles that indicate social class, education, and respect. Señor and Señora are always safe introductions, but when addressing your professional counterparts it is better to use a more specific title that refers to their professional accomplishments and status (see pages 146–7).

Using Don or Doña before someone's first name indicates respect and seniority with affection, and is usually used by someone of lower status to someone of higher status: storekeepers to address their patrons or secretaries to address their bosses. Highly skilled artisans, furniture makers, construction workers, and head workmen are *maestro*, a nod to expertise in their craft.

Su Merced

Listen closely and you will hear a very old and formal use of Spanish today in Bogotá, in the departments of Cundinamarca and Boyacá. You will be addressed as *su merced* (your mercy), an offering of the utmost respect and humility. If you are not paying attention you may miss it at first, as the locals say it so fast. Often shopkeepers and workmen employ it, as in "if your mercy would call the office and make the appointment." But if, like me, you are unfamiliar with it, you may be confused as to who is supposed to do what when the conversation is over!

INVITATIONS HOME

Once you have been introduced around you will certainly be invited to someone's home, as people entertain frequently. Upper-class Colombians do this in an "old world style," proper and elegant, following the rules of high society. Expect a long formal affair with fine china, silver service, and lace doilies. A lunch at someone's home may last three hours. These parties will be lovely but not opulent as upper-class Colombians are careful not to appear ostentatious or tacky by going overboard.

Entertaining for the middle class is not as formal or elegant as for their social superiors, depending largely on the type of event and the finances of the hosts. Often a dinner party will be a more casual affair—friends getting together, a buffet dinner. Guests will bring wine, beer, or whiskey and sometimes a dessert. Dancing or karaoke are popular.

Among the working and lower classes, entertaining is not always possible due to financial hardship. Sometimes it does not go beyond an invitation to the family dinner.

What Do I Bring?

The hostess takes responsibility for all of the preparations, so don't offer to bring a dish or a dessert unless you have been asked to do so—no potluck meals. A well mannered guest brings the hostess a gift—a bottle of wine, flowers, or chocolates are all appropriate. The day after a formal event guests might send flowers as a thank you.

What Do I Wear?

Colombians like to dress well and dress up. If a hostess says "casual" she means you don't have to come in a suit, not that you should wear jeans and tennis shoes. In Bogotá people wear stylish but conservative clothes.

They should never be revealing: an outfit that breaks this rule will raise eyebrows.

In Bogotá's fall-like weather women often wear pants, a stylish light coat, and a scarf or wrap. Men choose dark suits with pastel shirts and matching ties, or, for more relaxed gatherings, slacks and a sweater. Of course, in the warmer climates, people dress in lighter clothes—white linen, silk, and cotton—and will wear less. In Cartagena you won't look out of place if you wear a *guayabera*, an elegant pleated and embroidered linen or cotton shirt worn in all Caribbean countries from Mexico to Venezuela. In any location, when going to a Colombian home you should err on the dressy side.

TIMEKEEPING

Colombians run on "Colombian time" for social engagements, but have adopted American time *(en punto)* for more official matters—business meetings, doctor's appointments, plane and bus schedules, and the theater. This means that people might show up 9:00 p.m. or even later for an 8:00 p.m. invitation, but will arrive for a lunch meeting at the scheduled time.

No one agrees on what *"tiempo colombiano"* is, so things can get confusing: it can be anywhere from one to two hours late. Some hostesses pay attention to timekeeping; others might still be dressing when you arrive on time.

When the party starts you might be offered rounds of strong drinks, whiskey or rum, with no wine or finger foods available. The hostess may wait for everyone on *tiempo colombiano* to arrive before any food (at all) is served. But, be warned, if you arrive too late there may not be any food left! Colombian hostesses tend to measure portions based on how many guests are coming without adding in extras for unexpected guests (and people will bring unexpected guests) or for second helpings.

Hostess Tricks
Expatriate hostesses have gotten tricky with their invitations to combat *tiempo colombiano*. One friend confessed that when she invites both Colombians and foreigners to dinner she sends out two different invitations, inviting Colombians two hours earlier than foreigners. That way all the guests might arrive around the same time!

ROMANCE AND THE FOREIGNER

American men say that dating in Colombia does wonders for one's self-esteem. The ego boost comes from the special attention and warmth Colombian women show them, more than they might have received when they were back home. Colombian women are attentive and flirtatious, doting on the men they are dating, holding their hand freely, and calling them *mi amor* (my love). Colombian women are reputedly almost always ready to say "yes" to a date: men are rarely turned down, which of course feels good. Colombian women give gifts, call on the phone regularly, and are generous with hugs and kisses—it's in their nature. In spite of being a deeply Catholic country, Colombia is simply amorous.

The rules of dating differ in Colombia from other countries, which can lead to misunderstandings. Colombian women tend to approach a dating situation with unspoken expectations: usually hopes for something more serious. They tend to assume that the relationship has taken a more serious turn early on, calling someone *mi novio* (my boyfriend) after only a few dates. In contrast, by American standards a relationship takes longer to develop.

Some Colombian women are also more forward than women are in the USA. American men say that they are regularly asked out on dates, and often have their social calendar filled by plans women make for them, with little effort on their part. Both men and women have a more flexible approach to telling the truth or revealing personal details that a foreigner might consider pertinent, like that they have a boyfriend or are married. At the same time, the definition of "boyfriend" or "girlfriend" is looser than it is in the USA, and Colombians may be dating a number of other people while they have a "boyfriend."

Colombian men do not pursue foreign women to the same extent as Colombian women do foreign men, so, as a foreign women, you will have to make an effort on the dating scene and compete with local women. But, if you are a blonde traveling in Colombia, expect *a lot* of male attention.

Bending the Truth

An American friend was taken by surprise while on a date with a Colombian woman. After a great dinner, the two were in a taxi headed to go dancing when the woman answered a call on her cell phone. On the other end of the line was her boyfriend—whom my American friend had not known about. And when she told her boyfriend that she was out with girlfriends and on her way home, it rolled off her tongue so easily that it seemed that bending the truth was a normal part of life. After she hung up the phone, she continued on the date as if nothing had happened, no explanations apparently necessary!

HOMOSEXUALITY AND DISCRIMINATION

Homosexuality is not widely accepted in Colombia. Although it was decriminalized in 1980, and more recent legislative rulings have attempted to protect gay rights, there is no law preventing discrimination against homosexuals, and harassment and violence toward them is frequent. Even though the courts have made great efforts to protect rights on paper, there is still a long way to go in changing public opinion. In many places in Colombia it is not safe to be openly homosexual, and travelers should use caution when traveling outside cosmopolitan urban areas.

chapter five

THE COLOMBIANS AT HOME

As we have seen, mass urbanization and more than four decades of armed conflict have forced an estimated 3.5 million victims from their homes, many of whom have flooded Colombia's four major cities, Bogotá, Cali, Barranquilla, and Medellín. Today an estimated 70 percent of the population live in urban areas, many in slums and displacement settlements outside major cities.

The disparity between rich and poor in Colombia is enormous. As you can expect, Colombian daily life varies greatly depending on one's economic status, social class, and geographical location. Urban Colombians (excluding the very poor and displaced) enjoy modern conveniences that usually work well: sanitary arrangements, clean (potable) running water, electricity, trash collection, well maintained streets, good public transportation, telephone, and even the Internet (although short electrical outages are frequent even in Bogotá's wealthiest neighborhoods). But life in poor rural areas is not as easy. Many lack the most basic infrastructure and basic necessities like running water and electricity. The slums of Medellín and Barranquilla are some of the worst in Colombia.

Life in Colombia's rural peasant communities is a flashback to centuries past—peasants living in adobe cottages tending vegetable gardens or cooking in outdoor kitchens on wood-burning "stoves," using donkeys as labor to carry a load while herding animals along the side of the road. The difference between urban and rural life is extreme.

HOUSING

The Colombian home differs dramatically according to location and the elements—rainfall, temperature, and altitude—and the socioeconomic status of the owner. In the small villages that line jungle beaches in the

department of Chocó, there are open bamboo and wood structures with high thatched roofs protected from the elements under dense foliage fronting the shore. Beach houses in Tumaco in the department of Nariño are modest, built of wood plank, grayed by the sun and sea, elevated above the water on wooden stilts. In Tayrona National Park on the blistering Caribbean coast sit indigenous round houses: windowless, stone and *adobe*, topped with thatched roofs. Traditional *adobe* construction keeps the hot sun out and woven palm roofs provide natural ventilation.

In the coffee-growing region of Caldas, two-story wood and adobe farmhouses with flower hung balconies dot the landscape. Traditional homes in Colombia's mountain towns are built in the Andean vernacular—small windows, two-story thick adobe walls, and wood-burning fireplaces to ease the mountain chill. Cartagena's Spanish colonial homes, painted in pastels, open inward to elegant interior patios, letting in warm sunshine. And large rustic estates, *fincas* surrounded by coffee or pineapple plantations and stables, watch over the countryside waiting for weekend guests.

Urban homes differ greatly depending on the neighborhood and *estrato*. Bogotá's wealthy live in luxury apartments in sleek brick and glass high-rise, high security, buildings in the north with views of the city, and tree lined streets below. Building and garage access are controlled by around-the-clock *porteros,* doormen who act as both concierge and security guards. Residents come and go by car, often driven by a private driver/bodyguard, a holdover from the recent past when kidnappings were commonplace.

Garbage is collected from piles on the street once a week. But before the official garbage trucks arrive for their 3:00 a.m. pickup, the trash has already been picked over by scavenger families. *Recicladores,* some of the poorest (and most hardworking) families in the city, collect recyclables from city trash piles using horse drawn carts. In the most wealthy neighborhoods. outside the local supermarket you will find horses nibbling orange and banana rinds while their owners search for recyclables, and many Bogotá traffic jams can be traced to a plodding horse drawn cart!

Middle-class city dwellers live in older high-rise apartment complexes or two-story buildings in the center of the city. In Bogotá the working poor live in the south of the city, *El Sur*, in low-rise apartment complexes in tough neighborhoods not recommended to the visitor.

High above Bogotá and Medellín live the poorest residents, in dilapidated and dangerous cliffside slums with views of the wealthy neighborhoods below. Ramshackle multistory structures, with holes for windows and doors looking like they might wash down the hillside in the next rainstorm.

Empleadas

Most every wealthy Colombian household employs an *empleada* (or several), who does the cleaning, laundry, and ironing, and often cares for the children. If she has time she might also cook, do the grocery shopping, and pay utility bills at the bank. Upper-class Colombians consider it essential to have domestic help; it is not considered a luxury since good labor comes cheap. Daily wages for domestic help are significantly lower than in Europe or in the USA. Colombian maids and nannies tend to be knowledgeable, experienced, and extremely hardworking.

Many families with children choose a live-in, who sleeps at the residence. Others have day maids. In line with Colombia's strict class hierarchy, the family's relationship with the *empleada* is formal, even if she has worked with the same family for years and is regarded as part of the family. She always wears a uniform purchased by the employer.

Employers are required to pay overtime, severance pay, vacation pay, social security, and health care.

DAILY LIFE

> *Al que madruga, Dios le ayuda.*
> (Those who rise early, God will help).
> Colombian saying

Many Colombians come from poor backgrounds and have to work very hard to make ends meet. For many, daily existence is a challenge. The numbers of unemployed have increased as *desplacados* have flooded Colombia's cities looking for shelter and work.

Colombians come from the agrarian tradition of early rising and hard work and definitely do not fit the lazy Latin American stereotype. Urban people begin their workday early, sometimes leaving home at 6:00 a.m. or earlier to get to their office by 7:00 or 8:00 a.m. Breakfast is eaten at home, followed by traditional *media nueves* (half nines) and *onces* (elevens), snack times at the office.

Lunch begins early by Latin American standards, starting between 12:00 and 1:00 p.m. and lasting only an hour or two. Office workers take a quick lunch in a local restaurant. Professionals often have business lunches at nicer restaurants, taking an hour or so. Lunch is the main meal of the day and is heavier than in the USA or UK. No Colombian would dream of ordering just a salad for lunch!

Offices close at 5:00–5:30 p.m. but senior executives might stay at work until 7:00 p.m., maybe later. After work people might go for a coffee with colleagues or friends. Stores stay open until 7:30–8:00 p.m. Often people will stop at a supermarket or specialty store on the way home to pick up the makings for dinner and a much loved French baguette.

Colombians are starting to dine out much more than they used to, and good restaurants are opening to fill the demand. Friends will meet for dinner at a restaurant around 8:00 p.m., though Colombians do not go out to dinner every night. Generally people will eat a light dinner at home with their families.

The Legend of Onces

Colombians dispute the origin and even the definition of *onces* (literally, elevens — a snack between meals) or what time you are supposed to enjoy them. These are the traditional in-between meal times in Colombia and Chile, and are a South American mixture of the Spanish *merienda* and the English afternoon tea. Some say that *onces* are the mid-morning snack eaten between breakfast and lunch, after *media nueves* at 9:30 a.m. but before lunch, which seems understandable since they are called elevens. But maintain they really are the late afternoon snack, an interpretation of English teatime. But, then, why are elevens taken in the afternoon? Legend says that *"voy a tomar onces"* ("I am going to take/drink onces") is code for sneaking out for a nip, not of tea but of *aguardiente*, Colombia's local spirit, which has eleven (*once*) letters.

Daily Shopping

Large, US-style supermarkets and drugstores dominate the shopping experience in Colombia's major cities. Large chains provide one-stop convenience and secure garage parking, but convenience comes at a relatively high price.

Traditional *plazas del mercado* (market squares) still exist in working class neighborhoods and are where most

shopping is done in rural areas. Mom-and-pop produce stores dot the cities in some residential neighborhoods, and are mainstays in the countryside. Going to a *plaza del mercado*, especially Bogotá's enormous Paloquemao or Codabas market, is a great way for a visitor to experience local color and Colombia's long list of exotic fruits and flowers, but in wealthy urban neighborhoods traditional markets have been replaced by upscale supermarkets.

Most families do one large shopping run a week, and do quick pickups after work for extras. Many *empleadas* do the major shopping for their employers on weekday mornings. Street vending doesn't exist as much as in some Latin American countries, but in Bogotá street traders do brisk business selling avocados, strawberries, grapes, and mangos at corner stands.

GROWING UP IN COLOMBIA

The experience of childhood in Colombia depends largely on social class and economic means. Children from well-to-do families will have many more comforts than children from lower-class families—better and longer education, travel experiences, and leisure time. Lower-class families have a harder time getting by and often put their children to work from a young age instead of allowing them to finish school.

Children

Children in all classes are the center of family life and are truly adored. Upper-class families usually have a nanny to help raise the children, but the children still receive a lot of parental attention. Comfortably off families always have maids, so children are not required to help around the house. They receive a good education and most go to university, sometimes in the USA or Europe. Very wealthy children will spend vacations with family in the Colombian countryside at the family *finca*, or in the USA in Miami or New York. Usually children live at home with their parents until they are married.

In lower-class families, parents work long hours and have onerous city commutes, so they have to rely on siblings and grandparents to help with child care. Often these children have never traveled outside Colombia, and may never have left the city where they live. They will go to public schools and may well complete high school. Until recently, parents had to pay for public education, which resulted in low school enrollment in certain sectors. Today, more and more children enroll in secondary school since the government now subsidizes public education 100 percent.

Family Events

Family celebrations are an important part of Colombian life. The entire family, a large group of extended family, and friends gather to celebrate just about anything! Major events include baptisms and first communions, *quinceañeras*, and weddings.

Quinceañeras

The *quinceañera*, a tradition throughout Latin American, is a "sweet fifteen" birthday party, when the family throws their daughter an elaborate and expensive party—a rite of passage to celebrate the move into womanhood. The family takes months to prepare for the monumental event, and might have to save money for years to pay for it.

The *quinceañera* party is a momentous occasion in the life of a teenage girl. It is her coming out party. She spends hours on her hair and makeup, and wears a formal floor-length dress, often in a standout color like turquoise or fuchsia. She dances the first dance with her father. A live mariachi reggaeton band plays and everybody dances all night long.

Parents try to give their *quinceañera* a gift that will ensure her popularity and place in society. Even for working-class Colombians, a popular present these days is a one- to two-week cruise to Miami and the Bahamas. Many families save for year to pay for the big bash and the cruise, which can cost up to US$5,000. Cosmetic surgery is also, sadly, a common gift.

Weddings

In upper-class families, wedding festivities begin with six months of showers, country club luncheons, celebration dinners, and *finca* weekends in the country. Two nights before the wedding, the family hosts an elegant party called the *entrada de los regalos* (arrival of the gifts) at the bride's home. It is a formal party to which the guests (invited to attend the wedding in two days) come to deliver gifts. This event can be as expensive and elaborate as the wedding itself. Guests bring presents, but cash or gift certificates (*lluvia de sobres)* are considered in bad taste. The groom presents his bride with a *serenata*—a mariachi band at midnight.

Lower-class families celebrate weddings in as grand a way as the family can afford. Friends of the bride always throw the bride a wedding shower, *la despedida de soltera* (saying good-bye to being single), at which she receives household gifts. The friends of the groom take him out for a bachelor party, which involves a lot of drinking.

At a Catholic wedding the ceremony takes places in church, with a priest officiating. The *padrinos* (godparents) of the bride and groom accompany them to the altar, and the father of the bride "gives her away." Children have an active role in the ceremony, carrying the wedding ring and (in upper-class weddings) the *arras*—thirteen gold coins symbolizing a dowry—a tradition from colonial times.

Friends and family attend the church ceremony, then meet that evening (usually on Saturday) for the reception, usually held in a rented *salon de eventos*, a reception hall. In many cases, traditional Colombian foods like *lechona* (roast, stuffed pig) and *tamales*, or *arroz con pollo* (rice with chicken) are served in abundance, and wine, beer, and the favorite Colombian drinks like *aguardiente* and *chicha* flow (see page 117). Of course, there is music and dancing. A tall, layered wedding cake is served with champagne, and the guests toast the bride and groom. For lower-class weddings, guests bring gifts to the reception, often gift certificates or cash gifts.

MARRIAGE, DIVORCE, AND *UNIÓN LIBRE*

While civil marriages have been legal in Colombia since 1973 and are increasingly popular, many still consider a Catholic wedding more desirable. Parents try to give their children the most elaborate and elegant church wedding possible because of the attached implications of social status and wealth.

Divorce is possible only after civil marriage; there is no legal divorce after Catholic marriage. As more and more

people choose civil marriage, divorce is becoming more
common in Colombia. Women seem to be empowered by
the possibility of divorce. In the case of a breakdown of a
Catholic marriage, people stay married but separate and
often take up other families, a *unión libre.*

It seems contradictory for couples in a deeply Catholic
country to choose to be in a *unión libre*—a common-law
relationship in which couples live together, share financial
responsibilities, and raise children with no legal vows, but
the *unión libre* is increasingly popular. More conservative
Colombians feel the practice of *unión libre* is morally
wrong and is eating away at Colombian traditions,
revealing the tensions within a morally conservative
society that is changing rapidly.

EDUCATION

Colombians value education and intellectualism. The
country has a highly educated middle and upper class,
many of whom have been to the best schools in Colombia,
and in the USA and Europe. Excellent private schools and
universities exist in Colombia's large cities. It is essential
to be educated if one is upper class, as one's position in
society has more to do with education, culture, and
heritage than it does money. Education is also seen as a
means to socioeconomic advancement and a way to reduce
the ongoing insurgency and violence. Experts consider that
the lack of education in rural areas is a major contributing
factor to Colombia's armed conflict, in that without
education peasants are easily led by rebel groups, and
without access to education they feel disenfranchised and
are more willing to follow them.

Historically Colombia has struggled with educating its
rural population and keeping kids in school, but the Uribe
administration has made great improvements. They made
public school (grades 1–11) free, and school attendance is

up. Uribe focused funding on making the educational system more functional and more accessible to rural populations. Still, in 2009, while urban literacy is high at 91.6 percent, rural literacy is only 67 percent.

Preschool and *Jardin*

Many upper-class children attend preschool (*jardin*), starting as early as eighteen months, but most kids start kindergarten (*kinder*) at age four. *Jardines* in Bogotá are high quality and provide half-day educational child care. In private *jardines* it is not unusual to have a teacher for every three to six children.

Grade School and High School (Grades 1–11)

Nine years of compulsory schooling start with elementary school at age six, although in some rural areas only five years of schooling are required. Families can choose free public schooling (*colegio distrital*), but those who can afford it choose private schools, which offer foreign language programs, the Advanced Placement system or the International Baccalaureate syllabus, and often programs for students with special needs. All schools require students to wear uniforms purchased by the parents.

Primary school (*primaria*) grades 1 to 5 run on half-day schedules, either 7:00 to 12:00 a.m. or 2:30 to 6:00 p.m. Secondary school (*bachillerato*) grades 6 to 11 begin at 7:00 or 8:00 a.m. and run until early afternoon. Major vacations are a long Christmas break from mid-December to February, a vacation in June, as well as a fall break in October, and Semana Santa.

University

More and more Colombians are receiving higher education, many of them women. Colombia has over 375 institutions of higher learning, including public and

world-class private universities. Bogotá has some of the oldest and most esteemed universities in the country, as well as the largest public university, Universidad Nacional de Colombia, which also has campuses in Medellín, Manizales, and Palmira. Both the Universidad de los Andes in Bogotá and the Universidad del Valle in Cali are internationally recognized for their academic excellence.

Students graduate high school (grade 11) at sixteen and most usually begin college right away. Most complete college when they are twenty or twenty-one years old, early by US standards. The elite might go to the USA or Europe for university. Engineering, economics, law, and medicine are popular degree choices.

MILITARY SERVICE

Colombia's military—the armed forces, the army, navy, and coast guard, and the air force—is under the command of the president. All of these forces, along with the Civil Defense and the National Police, are part of the Ministry of Defense and are governed by a civilian minister of defense.

Colombia requires all male nonstudents aged eighteen to twenty-four to do eighteen to twenty-four months' compulsory service in the armed forces. Those with a high school diploma are exempt from combat. Men and women aged eighteen to forty-nine are eligible for voluntary enlistment. Women today play an active role in the armed forces, some in high ranking positions, but are not required to serve by law. Young men are drafted by what is supposed to be a random lottery conducted by municipality, but data reveals that not all sectors of society are called up equally. The majority of conscripts come from uneducated lower-class backgrounds, and those from wealthy backgrounds often buy their way out of the draft.

HEALTH INSURANCE

Colombia has an advanced multitiered health care system, with coverage across all sectors of society. The 1993 health care reform increased health coverage from 28 percent of the population (pre-1993) to more than 66 percent today, and today HIV/AIDS, cancer, and cardiovascular disease are covered. For the very poor the government subsidizes health coverage. Foreign and domestic companies are required to contribute to health plans to share costs with employees.

chapter six

TIME OUT

LEISURE TIME

Colombians spend their leisure time with family and close friends, whether on vacation or at home. They are very gregarious and love having people around. Most gatherings center on a big party or a meal. There are always dinner parties—there doesn't need to be a reason to entertain.

Colombians are hard workers, and put in a lot of hours at the office. There is little downtime, given long hours and tough commutes in clogged city traffic, certainly no midday *siesta* or relaxing lunch at home. Office workers legally have ten vacation days per year, but with national holidays, vacation days add up to many more than this. The long list of national holidays and subsequent Mondays off work are welcome breaks in busy lives. Anyone with the cash heads out to a *finca* (if you don't own, you rent) with family and friends—*the* Colombian way to spend the weekend. For longer vacations, the super wealthy head to the airport for a short flight to Miami. Working- and lower-class Colombians often don't have the extra money to leave town on vacation, so they spend time with their families at home. For this hardworking group, free time is mostly devoted to chores rather than leisure. When funds allow, families visit relatives in other *pueblos*. Over Christmas the upper and middle classes take monthlong vacations, as cities virtually shut down—schools are out, and stores, hotels, restaurants, *and* the government close for *vacaciones collectivas*.

On weekends entire families head off to quaint nearby towns *de paseo* (taking a stroll) to enjoy Colombia's pastoral charms, or drive to the country to feast at a traditional *asadero* (barbeque restaurant). If it is raining, many families head to upscale malls for shopping and playtime with the kids (malls in Colombia have play areas for young children and special ones for babies).

FOOD IN COLOMBIA

The many cuisines of Colombia all reflect, to different degrees, its ethnic diversity and unique geography. Much of the country is devoted to agriculture, and with its location near the equator the growing season lasts

all year-long. Market stalls overflow with the local bounty—grass fed beef, fresh vegetables, and tropical

fruits—every month of the year. Recently there has been a culinary awakening in Colombia's major cities: chefs are celebrating Colombian flavors and products in creative new ways—think mango tart or plantain gnocchi.

Colombian food, for the most part, is peasant fare, simply prepared and gently flavored using local ingredients. People have a passion for red meat grilled over a wood-

burning fire, served plain—no sauce, with grilled corn and potatoes on the side. The food varies dramatically by region. On the highland plateau Spanish influences meet Andean flavors in hearty soups filled with meats, potatoes, and corn, enjoyed with a few glasses of South American red wine or a cold beer. Paisa food, in and around Medellín, is heavy on beans and sausage. Costeño food, from the coast, marries Spanish and African flavors with native tropical ingredients—fresh fish and *mariscos* (shellfish,) coconut, *yuca*, rice, tropical fruits, and plantains. No meal is complete without *arepas* (Colombia's version of tortillas) and a cup of smooth Colombian *tinto*, black coffee.

At the market you will encounter strange tubers and exotic fruits. From the *tierra caliente* come an array of tropical fruits like *platano, lulo, uchuva, guanábana,* and *guayaba*. Make sure to try the local potatoes, *papas criollas*: they are something special. It being the Andes, potatoes are a staple, along with corn and pumpkin. But you might be surprised by how much rice you will eat in Colombia. Nowhere else in South America is rice so important to the cuisine.

Street food favorites are fresh mango and avocado. Mango sellers fill plastic bags with mango chunks, either *verde* (green) or *maduro* (ripe). Avocado venders sell enormous sweet Papelillo avocados from street side stands, sliced in half and eaten with a sprinkle of salt.

Mealtimes

Breakfast *(desayuno)* is a large meal eaten early, a holdover from agrarian traditions. A city breakfast might include eggs and cheese or *calentado* (fried rice with beans, meat, and sometimes plantain), bread or *arepa*, juice or fruit, accompanied by coffee or hot chocolate and is often followed by a mid-morning snack *(onces)*. In rural areas breakfast is bigger still, and might include *envueltos* or *tamales* (corn dough stuffed with cheese or meats, steamed in a corn husk). In Antioquia, the *bandeja paisa*, consisting of ground beef, sausage, *arepa*, *chicharron* (fried pork skin), rice, and beans, topped with a fried egg, will keep you going until dinner!

Lunch *(almuerzo)* is the main meal of the day. As in much of Latin America, it tends to be a heavier meal than in the USA. It might start with a light soup, then a piece

of grilled meat served with potatoes, rice and, *arepas,* followed by dessert or fruit and coffee. Or it may be a large bowl of one of Colombia's hearty soups like *ajiaco* or *sancocho,* complete meals in themselves. In working-class areas and in small towns, the place to go for a true Colombian home cooked meal is the corner *corrientazo* (literally an electric shock), a local lunch spot that serves up a fixed price menu loaded with meat and enough carbs to electrify your body with energy to keep you going for days. Most office workers go out for lunch these days. Construction workers bring their lunches to work and can be seen lounging in the park eating from stacked tin trays of home cooked fare. Families often go out for a long Sunday meal, which becomes the afternoon activity.

Generally, supper *(cena)* is a lighter meal than breakfast or lunch. Colombians at home might eat a salad and a sandwich or soup. At the same time, many are choosing to go out to dinner.

Eating Out

The "going out to eat" culture is growing in major cities and chefs are responding, with new restaurants opening all the time. As the middle class expands, more people are eating out. Excellent restaurants in Bogotá, Cartagena, and Medellín serve haute cuisine at very affordable prices. In European style, chefs offer special tasting menus with 5 to 20 (gasp!) courses to showcase their specialties, often paired with wines. Bogotá and Medellín are beginning to be recognized as foodie destinations. It's a good time to eat out in Colombia!

Vegetarians will have a difficult time finding something meat-free in restaurants serving Colombian food and in small towns, but in major cities there are plenty of Asian and Mediterranean options that will appeal to them.

Colombian Specialties

Ajiaco Santafereño

The true flavor of the *altiplano* and Bogotá's most famous
dish, this chicken and potato stew wards off the chill of
the high plains. This stew's indigenous origins have over
time been adapted to European tastes, making it a true
fusion dish. Fresh chicken
is boiled slowly with slices
of chewy Andean corn and
three varieties (no less) of
Andean potatoes until the
stew becomes thick and
creamy. Fresh *guascas*, a
wild herb native to the
Andes, gives *ajiaco* its
unique flavor. Originally a

spoon of *ají* (chile sauce) added spicy heat, giving the stew
its name, but today it is finished instead with ingredients
from the Spanish kitchen, salty capers and a dollop of
heavy cream.

Sancocho

Sancocho is Colombia's other famous soup; it is a Spanish
cocido reinvented. The Spanish brought *cocido* (a boiled

peasant meal of meat, cabbage, and garbanzo beans) to Colombia, and Colombians made it their own using local ingredients and a tropical touch. Most every region and every cook has their own recipe for *sancocho*. Cauca's is a slowly cooked chicken and oxtail stew with plantains, *yuca*, pumpkin, and corn. Costeño *sancocho* is rich with coconut milk and filled with fresh fish and vegetables of the *tierra caliente*—sweet plantains, *yuca*, and the enormous potato-like root *ñame*.

Comida Costeña

The cuisine of Colombia's Caribbean and Pacific coasts reflects the unique cultural diversity of the region, a mix of Spanish, indigenous, and African culinary traditions using tropical ingredients—with delicious results. Fresh fish, *langostinos* and *caracoles* (large shrimp and snails) are the stars, often sautéed in thick and rich coconut milk, wrapped in a banana leaf and steamed until just tender. Many dishes use coconut milk as a base— *gallina* (chicken) *al coco, arroz con coco,* and *langostinos encocados* —large shrimp cooked in thick coconut milk.

Lechona

Lechona is Tolima's celebration of the pig. Along with *ajiaco, lechona* might be Colombia's most famous dish. Making *lechona* is a labor of love, taking two to three days for the entire process. A whole pig is emptied out—bones, meat, and all—then stuffed with seasoned shredded pork and dried peas. The virtue of adding rice is hotly contested. The entire pig skin is then rubbed with an *adobo,* a spice rub of cumin, salt, pepper, and bitter orange juice, and slow roasted in a brick oven overnight, for twelve hours. If you don't make it to Tolima to try the original, you'll still be able to taste it in Bogotá, where *lechona tolimense* and *tamales tolimenses* are popular party foods that serve a big crowd.

Empanadas

Empanadas are a South American favorite, but what makes the Colombian versions unique are their small size and their great crunch—results of skilled hands and the corn dough that is fried until crisp and golden. *Empanadas bogotanas* have an Andean twist: filled with stewed beef and local potatoes. On the coast, *empanadas* are sold as street food in the local plaza.

Arepas

No Colombian meal is complete without Colombia's favorite ground corn flat bread, the *arepa*. These ubiquitous corn patties are grilled plain, or filled with cheese. Costeño *arepas* somehow contain an egg (how *do* they get that egg inside?) and are then fried golden, a true delight

Envueltos de Mazorca

Every few steps in the *mercado* you will find a woman selling *envueltos*, Colombia's fresh corn *tamales*. Wrapped tightly in fresh corn husks, they are small and compact—the perfect market snack. In rural areas Colombian's eat *envueltos* at breakfast. Some *envueltos* are *dulce* (sweet): fresh corn blended with *cuajada* (fresh milk curd cheese), raisins, and a pinch of sugar. Others are *salado* (savory), made with ground fresh corn, butter, *cuajada*, and salt.

Meat

To many, Sunday means a day in the country at a barbeque restaurant (*asadero*) feasting on grilled meat. Colombians like their meat grilled on a *parilla* (iron barbeque grill) over a hot wood fire, and served with a choice of Colombian standards: *arepas, papas criollas o saladas, yuca,* and *mazorca* (grilled corn on the cob.) It is a meat-lover's delight. No room is "wasted" on salads at an *asadero*.

An *asadero* lunch is an assortment of *carne de res* (beef),

lomo de cerdo (pork loin), *costillas de cerdo* (pork ribs), *pollo* (chicken), *longaniza* (smoked sausages), *chorizo* (fresh sausages), and *morcilla* (blood sausages filled with rice), with *guacamole* (avocado sauce), and *ají* (chile sauce) on the side.

A little bit of everything is served family style on one big platter, and everyone dives in with their fingers.

BEEF THE WAY YOU WANT IT

When ordering beef at an *asadero* you may not have a choice of how it is cooked —it is usually medium well. Colombian beef is very lean, so it is cut thin to keep it tender, and on the grill it is hard to control the doneness. But in restaurants devoted to beef, you will be asked *"Qué termino?"* "How would you like your meat cooked?" If you prefer your meat medium in the USA, this is not the same as *"medio"* in Colombia. A steak cooked *"medio"* will arrive rare and very red in the center, so if you like medium, ask for *"tres cuartos."'* (Meats other than beef are cooked medium-well to well done.)

Here are the popular Colombian cuts of beef and the possible ways you can have them cooked.

CORTES DE RES: CUTS OF BEEF
Lomo de Res: Filet of beef
Chata or Churrasco: New York steak
Punto de Anca: Top sirloin cap or tri-tip steak

LOS TERMINOS: DONENESS OF THE MEAT
A Punto/Bleu: Very rare/blue and cold in the center
Medio: Medium rare to rare/red and warm in the center
Tres Cuartos: Medium/pink in the center
Bien Cocida: Well done

Tropical Fruits

Colombia has a wild array of tropical fruits. Fresh fruit is eaten for breakfast, as a street snack or pureed into *jugos,* juices thinned with water or milk. There are the usual suspects—bananas, papayas, pineapples, and mangos. Going beyond the standards, there are many more! *Lulo* is a favorite for juice, orange on the outside and bright green inside; it tastes like tangerine spiked with lime and pineapple. *Maracuya*, or passion fruit, looks like an ostrich egg. A ripe *maracuya* has shriveled skin that makes it look rotten but inside gelatinous bubbles of passion fruit juice nestle together like cells. *Guanábana* looks mean but tastes sweet! Its enormous spiky green armor hides pure white and sweet custardlike flesh.

Colombia's hot regions supply the world with most of its *platanos* (plantains), starchy oversized banana-like fruits, so if you feel you are seeing them everywhere, you are! *Platanos* are eaten ripe and green, sometimes mashed and often fried. Without knowing it, you will become a *platano* convert after just a few days in Colombia.

Andean Tubers

Andean potatoes and native tubers grow well from Colombia into Peru and Chile. Three varieties of potatoes, *criollas, sabaneras,* and *pastusas,* are staples in the Colombian kitchen.

Alongside Colombia's potatoes you will see baskets filled with odd-looking tubers native to the Andes. Make sure to take a look—they are interesting and rare! *Hibias,* white corkscrew-shaped roots, are a local favorite in Boyacá, where they are served broiled with melted cheese. *Cubios* are small, round, and red and look a little like new potatoes, but taste more like a radish. They are added to *piquete bogotano* (another Spanish *cocido* variation).

Arracacha and yuca are other Andean tubers with barklike skin and starchy flesh. Both are added to soups or made into chips.

Desserts

Colombian desserts do not play a big role in the local cuisine, but there are a few that people enjoy. You will find *oblea* stands selling paper-thin, crisp waffle cookies filled with *arequipe* or jam, a dessert sandwich. *Arequipe* is Colombia's *dulce de leche,* a burnt sweet milk similar to a sweet caramel sauce, an Old World recipe brought by the Spanish. *Cuajada* cheese is baked and served with a *panela* or fruit sauce. *Merengón,* a large meringue shell filled with fruit and whipped cream, also commands roadside stands.

YET MORE SPECIALTIES

Patacones: crispy flat green plantain disks served with *guacamole* or *hogao* (a thick tomato and onion sauce) and *suero* (thick soured cream) for dipping. Also served with *cebiche* (lime marinated seafood) as crackers.

Cebiche: Colombians enjoy *cebiche* in coastal regions where seafood is very fresh. Colombian *cebiche* is shrimp or raw fish marinated in lime and orange juice, sugar, spicy *ají criollo*, tomatoes, onions, and cilantro, or in coconut milk and lime.

Arroz con Coco: rice cooked with slivers of toasted coconut. Often topped with shrimp in a coconut sauce *(langostinos encocolados).*

Tamales Tolimenses: banana leaf bundles filled with a corn flour *masa* (dough), rice, peas, garbanzo beans, pork, and chicken, then submerged in water, and boiled until tender. This unique cooking method keeps the dough very moist.

Pastel de Carne or Pollo: savory turnovers with a flaky puff pastry dough and a simple meat or cheese filling.

Fritanga: all aspects of the pig—many cuts of pork fried in pork lard—*costillas* (ribs), *lomo* (loin), *chicharron* (pork fat and skin), and *oreja* (ear), along with *morcilla* (blood sausage), *longaniza* and *chorizo* sausage, and *chonchullo* (intestine).

WHAT'S TO DRINK?

The most famous Colombian drink is, of course, coffee. Smooth and full-bodied, Colombian coffee is a good blend of acidity and richness. Coffee is grown in the Zona Cafetera region south of Medellín in the fertile valley between the Cordillera Occidental and the Cordillera Central. Colombians enjoy *un tinto* (black coffee) anytime of the day. If you want your coffee with milk, order a *café con leche* but expect more milk than coffee!

The two major coffee retailers, Oma and Juan Valdez, serve "lattes" and "cappuccinos" with *leche descremada* (nonfat milk,) a rarity in other Latin American countries. Many Colombians use *leche deslactosada* (lactose free milk), so if you want "nonfat" and not "lactose free," make sure to enunciate!

Colombians love whiskey—Scotch whisky, not bourbon. This is an upscale drink, served on the rocks at cocktail time. Sometimes you will be offered whiskey (occasionally rum) at a party and nothing else! But, being in South America, wine is popular in upper- and middle-class circles. Some chic wine bars in Bogotá serve more than forty wines by the glass and offer monthly wine tastings featuring wines from Chile, Argentina, and Spain.

A cold *cerveza* (beer) might be Colombia's favorite drink. A beer is refreshing in Colombia's overall hot climate and the perfect complement to the meaty food. Bavaria, Colombia's only industrial scale brewery, makes about five beers, all marketed to different sectors of the population. Aguila is the nation's best seller, while Poker is the lowest priced. Club Colombia is considered the premium. Bogotá's excellent microbrewery Bogota Beer Company, with pubs all over the city, brews on a small (and high quality) scale, and offers selections for every taste. And, you can have cases of beer, kegs (or mini-kegs), delivered to your house.

Colombia has its own *gaseosa* (soda)—a tamarind flavored cream soda called Colombiana. No *parilla* meal is complete without a *refajo*, a combination of beer and soda, usually Colombiana, definitely an acquired taste.

Anywhere there is sugarcane there will be rum, and Colombia is no exception. Santa Fe de Bogotá is a well respected bottle (or box—you can buy your rum in a box for easy travel!). *Aguardiente,* a popular anise-flavored sugarcane brandy, is Colombia's heavy hitting spirit.

The availability and low cost of tropical fruits make fruit juices as common as water in Colombia. *Moras* (blackberries) and *fresas* (strawberries) are so affordable that they make juice out of them! *Salpicón,* a juice of chopped fruits, made with papaya, banana, and pineapple, is like a drinkable (and refreshing) fruit salad.

Chicha, the indigenous beer of the Andes, has made a comeback in urban Bogotá. It is a fermented corn brew, slightly bubbly, thick, and yellow.

Un Tinto

In Colombia, if you ask for *un tinto*, you will get a cup of black coffee, but if you do the same in Mexico, you will get a glass of red wine—both fine choices, in my opinion, but not interchangeable!

SPORTS

Urban Colombians are active, sporty people. They go to the gym, play tennis, swim, and do triathlons, and they are serious about cycling. To a lot of people, Sunday in Bogotá means jump on your bike and ride. Public aerobics classes are given in Bogotá parks on Sundays, attracting hundreds of spandex clad enthusiasts.

You might not consider chugging beer and exploding things a "sport," but Colombians do. The game of *tejo* has been declared a national sport. It is played in the back of local *cantinas*, where, after consuming a good quantity of beer, you throw disks at gunpowder filled triangular targets. Of course, if your aim is good you'll know by the explosion.

Soccer

Colombians are fanatical *fútbol* (soccer) fans. People are devoted to their local teams and their passionate support is often an expression of regional rivalry. Colombia furiously tries to qualify for the World Cup, but doesn't usually make it. Nevertheless, the country comes to a standstill when it is World Cup time, and everyone watches obsessively.

Cycling

Many Colombians have a passion for cycling. Bogotá is one of the world's most bicycle friendly cities. In Medellín and Bogotá, Sundays mean Ciclovia, when the cities close major streets to cars and open them to cyclists, rollerbladers, roller skaters, and walkers. The Tour de Colombia, the national cycling competition, starts in March and goes on for twelve days. Mountainous terrain and high altitude make a perfect (if strenuous) training ground for cyclists. Even though it rains more than 180 days a year, Bogotanos are outdoors riding their bikes, rain or shine.

CULTURAL ACTIVITIES

A surprising amount of cultural activities are on offer
in Colombia's big cities. Bogotá is a cosmopolitan city
that plays host to international theater, music, and
film festivals. The upper class is highly educated,
sophisticated, and well traveled, so their expectations
are high—and Bogotá artists deliver. As Colombians
try to make sense of their recent political and social
conflict, there has been an explosion of cultural
expression in the arts, in the theater, and in the fine arts.

Teatro Colón, recently restored, is a nineteenth-
century architectural gem, a beautiful place to see
current opera and drama productions. The Teatro Jorge
Eliecer Gailán is a historic art deco theater that shows
contemporary dance and music productions. Biblioteca
Luis Angel Arango offers
art exhibits, concerts by
international and local artists,
and educational conferences,
plus poetry readings, a young
artists' program, as well
as weekend productions
designed for children. Every
two years, in April, is Bogotá's
international theater festival
extravaganza, the Festival
Iboamericano del Teatro.
September brings opera
season, and Bogotá's film
festival begins in October.

See www.bogotadc.com/eventos for current listings.

Bogotá's Musco del Oro tells the story of Colombia's
indigenous peoples through their passion for gold, and
houses a collection of thousands of pieces of jewelry and
ceremonial objects—definitely worth a visit. Also a must
is the Museo Botero. Housed in a restored mansion in

the historic La Candelaria neighborhood, the museum shows Fernando Botero's own collection of paintings by European masters (Picasso, Chagall, Miró, Monet, and more) donated by the Medellín native himself, as well as more than one hundred of his own works. Other museums

of note are the Museo de Arte Colonial, and the Museo Nacional and the Museo de Arte Moderno, which both feature Colombian artists heavily. In Medellín's Plaza Botero, the voluptuous bronze Botero sculptures stand proud in a public courtyard. Nearby, more than one hundred of his paintings and drawings are displayed in the Museo Antioquia.

Gabriel García Márquez

Gabo, as he is lovingly called, is Colombia's most acclaimed literary figure. Born in 1927 in the

small Caribbean town of Aracataca, he became an acclaimed journalist, nonfiction writer, novelist, and short story author. In 1982 he won the Nobel Prize for Literature, which launched him into international stardom. Many credit him with breathing new life into Latin American literature.

Some of Gabriel García Márquez's early novels use a journalistic style to chronicle the realities of everyday life in Colombia. Later novels and short stories employ a unique style that combines the fantastic and the realistic worlds to reflect the Colombian conscience, a world of "magical realism."

Márquez says the role of a good writer is to penetrate reality and expose the other side. In his most famous work, *One Hundred Years of Solitude*, he does just that. His narrative exists in a different reality, one that unsentimentally floats between the rationalism of everyday life and a spiritual magical world. Gabo's writing inspires strong feelings; some revere him as a literary genius, others find it an acquired taste. You can decide for yourself by starting with his most famous novels, *Love in the Time of Cholera* and *The General in his Labyrinth*. For a matter-of-fact account of Bogotá's terror filled 1990s, read *News of a Kidnapping*.

NIGHTLIFE

Colombians love to party, but none can top the Costeños' reputation as party animals! You will find a happening nightlife scene—bars, clubs, dance clubs—in all of Colombia's major cities. Medellín's El Poblado district is a barhopper's delight, with choices to suit every taste—beer saloons, champagne and wine bars, and vodka lounges.

Bogotá's night scene is lively most nights of the week. Whether you are looking for a hipster cocktail lounge or a glass of wine on a rooftop terrace with city views, you'll find it in the capital. The Zona "T" and Parque 93 are packed on weekends with young people, flaunting designer handbags and high heeled boots, out on the town.

Cali is Colombia's salsa city, so dust off your dancing shoes! Salsa music might have originated in Puerto Rico, but Cali has taken over salsa dancing rights! After

midnight Caleños (people from Cali) head to the dozens
of salsa clubs in the Juanchito district where they keep it
swinging all night long.

As in any big city, in all Colombian cities it's essential to
have your wits about you while out on the town. Always
keep your eye on your drink so that no one slips drugs
into it. Beware of teams who prey on the unassuming or
intoxicated. (For more on safety, see page 140.)

SHOPPING FOR PLEASURE

Shopping for pleasure is a major pastime among the upper
and middle classes. Upscale shopping malls dot major
cities, full of brand-name retail shops that do a brisk
business. Colombians like to stay current with the latest
fashions—designer labels matter. They spend as much on
fashion as the Italians and the French.

High fashion boutiques line Calles 83 and 84 at Carrera
14 in the Zona "T" in Bogotá. Three modern shopping
malls are popular in Bogotá: Andino mall in Zona "T"
(complete with kiddie play area, movie theater. and
casino), as well as the mega-mall Palatino and Hacienda
Santa Bárbara (Carrera 7 No. 115-60), an old hacienda
turned retail center in Usaquén. US and European brands
are expensive, even more so after the 16 percent value-
added tax is tacked on, but Colombians are willing to pay.

Medellín has the largest retail industry in Colombia.
Some visitors head there purely to shop in sparkling new
shopping malls that house the best designer boutiques.
Both Colombians and foreigners flock to Medellín for the
annual ColombiaModa fashion extravaganza in August,
the biggest fashion event in all of South America.

Others come to Colombia for its world famous
emeralds. They are the best value in Bogotá, but you have
to buy from a reputable dealer. Some dealers make emerald
shopping easy for you; they will come to your hotel or

home and show you loose stones, then set them for you. Your embassy may have a list of recommended dealers.

While in Bogotá don't forget the "leather district," which is a bargain for ready-made and custom-made handbags and boots, a must for the *Cachaca* (Bogotá woman). Many shops will custom make any style you want from a picture, so come prepared.

Artesanía (craft work) is not as abundant in Colombia as in other Latin countries, but there are some unique and well crafted pieces on offer. The standout is the Werregue basket, an intricate weaving tradition of Afro-Colombians from the Pacific rain forest region. Their graphic designs have been handed down from African basket weaving traditions. The weaving is so tight that these baskets were originally used to carry water. They have been described as the most perfect

and the most elegant expressions of *artesanía* made of fiber. Other items of note are the traditional black polished pottery from Tolima, *mola* appliqués (colorful sewn fabrics made by Colombia's Kuna people), handmade hammocks, Caribbean

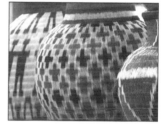

guayaberas (hand pleated and embroidered men's shirts), and handmade *vueltiao* (wide-brimmed straw) hats.

In Bogotá, Expoartesanías at Corferias in December, is Colombia's best (and largest) handicraft fair, and has abundant supplies of the best *artesanía* from many regions of Colombia, including pottery, basketry, leather goods, fashion, furniture, and jewelry.

Major credit cards are accepted at all major shopping malls and most retail stores, grocery stores, and higher end locations. Banks with ATMs are easy to find in major cities, in banks as well as in grocery stores and shopping malls. In handicraft markets and in small towns you will probably have to pay in cash.

> ### ARTESANÍA—WHAT TO BUY WHERE
> **Bogotá**—emeralds, black pottery, Wayuu colorful woven purses, *molas*, Werregue woven baskets, leather jackets, handbags, and boots
> **Ráquira**—terra-cotta pottery and hammocks
> **Monguí**—handmade leather soccer balls
> **Paipa**—handwoven hammocks
> **Nobsa**—lambs-wool *ruanas* (Andean cloaks) and thick lambs-wool blankets
> **Cartagena and Barranquilla**—tortoise shell jewelry, *guayaberas*, and *sombreros vueltiao*, woven, wide-brimmed hat made of cane straw, traditionally worn while dancing the *cumbia* and by Vallenato bands, now a symbol of Colombian culture

PLACES TO VISIT
Bogotá

For years Bogotá's reputation as a dangerous city has caused visitors to stay away. But today things are changing. Now, it is becoming a secret gem that remains mostly undiscovered by travelers. Although not the prettiest city in Latin America, Bogotá is vibrant, forward thinking and First World, alive with artistic inspiration, creativity, intellectual life, and urban progress. The location is stunning: it is a modern city nestled high in the Andes with its soaring green mountains always in view. As urban areas go, Bogota is small and manageable, while the cultural offerings exceed most cities twice its size.

In contrast to Bogotá's overall contemporary feel, La Candelaria, its still functioning sixteenth-century Spanish colonial center, is the best preserved and perhaps the most beautiful in Latin America. Charming small museums fill restored colonial mansions, whose ornately carved wooden balconies overlook narrow hillside cobblestoned streets.

Bogotá has redefined itself; now, cosmopolitan Bogotanos are out and about, enjoying their city—the designer shopping districts, the artsy Macarena district, neighborhood wine bars and chic restaurants, pedestrian areas, bicycle paths, and the many parks and outdoor events it has to offer. See www.bogota-dc.com/eventos/eventos.html for a list of current events.

For magnificent panoramic views of the city, take the *teleférico* (cable car) to the top of Cerro de Monserrate to the church that crowns the summit. If historic houses interest you, check out the 1820s home and gardens of The Liberator Simón Bolívar, Museo Quinta de Bolívar, nestled into the forest at the base of Cerro de Monserrate.

On Sundays, shoppers flock to Usaquén to the outdoor market with stalls filled with *artesanía*, then stroll through the historic *plaza principal* and stop for a relaxing lunch.

Outside Bogotá

Many quaint rural towns lie to the north of the capital and make a good day or overnight trip. The bucolic landscapes of Cundinamarca and Boyacá alone make the journey worthwhile—emerald green mountains dotted with small hamlets and grazing cattle. The colonial town of Tabio, 23 miles (38 km) north of Bogotá, is a good place to *pasear* like Colombians do, to stroll the historic cobblestone streets and plaza and lunch with the locals.

Farther north, about four hours north of Bogotá, you'll find Villa de Leyva, a quiet weekend retreat in a charming colonial village, with *hospederías* and *hostelerías* (small and large inns) to suit every taste. On the way you will pass Ubaté, where the cow population is greater than the human, accounting for the many artisanal cheese shops.

To the west of Villa de Leyva, the sixteenth-century mountain town of Monguí is rich in colonial charm. Residents still keep donkeys in their yards for transport and to assist in tilling the soil. Roosters and barking dogs add up to a full night's entertainment. On the way to Monguí, you will pass through Nobsa, famous for weaving traditional lambs-wool *ruanas* (Andean cloaks). Lago de Tota is picturesque and might make you hungry; this high elevation interior lake features on one side a peasant village that grows onions along the lakeshore, giving the air a fragrant aroma that awakens a craving for lunch. Guides in Monguí's main plaza (called *el parque* in these parts) offer guided tours to El Páramo de Ocetá, considered Colombia's most beautiful high altitude wetlands, located outside town. If white-water rafting is more your speed, head to San Gil, Colombia's adventure sports capital.

Cartagena

The Caribbean "walled city" is Colombia's colonial gem. The massive fortifications that the Spanish built to protect the city are in good condition today, and have been declared a

UNESCO World Heritage site. The narrow streets of the old city are lined with Spanish colonial houses, painted the colors of tropical fruits. Wooden balconies hang over the

streets, covered with flowering vines.

The pace is slow and relaxed in the heat of the day, but when the sun sets Latin rhythms and African beats fill the night air. To really feel Cartagena's charms, stay inside the walls of the ancient city where you'll find small boutique hotels with rooftop pools and city views, and beautifully restored seventeenth-century convents. Try the street food for local flavor—exotic fruit cocktails, freshly fried plantains, *cebiche* bathed in coconut milk, or spiny lobster tails with a squeeze of lime, all from the corner stand.

Zona Cafetera

Colombia's famed coffee grows in the fertile valley nested between the Cordillera Occidental and the Cordillera Central. This lush paradise is thick with coffee, banana, and pineapple plantations. Small farms and cheerful country houses dot the landscape. Three towns, Armenia, Pereira, and Manizales, make up the Zona Cafetera, each with their own airport. Flying in from Bogotá is easy, and many hotels will pick you up from the plane. Or, you can rent a car because driving from town to town is easy and considered safe. The pleasure of the Zona Cafetera is the landscape itself, so relax with a cup of local brew and take in the view.

chapter seven

TRAVEL, HEALTH, & SAFETY

GETTING AROUND SAFELY

The easiest, fastest, and safest way to travel around Colombia is by plane. Many road routes are considered safe, but driving through certain areas is putting yourself in harm's way. In some areas you risk inadvertently driving into insurgent territory and making yourself a target for kidnapping or worse. Residual land mines from the armed conflict continue to cause injuries and deaths, so venturing into rural areas can be dangerous in itself. The security condition fluctuates, and unless you are certain that the route is safe, it is just best to fly.

That said, driving in safe areas is surprisingly easy and pleasant. The government has made great efforts to protect certain roadways by increasing military presence and installing permanent checkpoints. The emerald green rolling hills outside Bogotá are spectacularly beautiful. Roads are mostly well maintained and signage is excellent, so good in fact that often you do not need to consult the map! Certain areas have not been affected by the trouble, and Colombians regularly drive around the countryside without a problem. So, if you want to drive, check with your embassy for a list of safe driving destinations before you head off. For your own safety, drive during daylight hours only.

BY AIR

Convenience, ease, and security make flying the best option for getting around. There are direct flights from Miami to all major cities, with most other international flights landing in Bogotá. Avianca airlines, a Delta partner, is the major provider for international and domestic flights, while two domestic airlines, Aires and AeroRepublica, fly to many smaller cities at discounted fares. Make sure to book in advance as tickets go up in price the closer to your travel date, especially if you are traveling over Semana Santa and Christmas.

ON THE ROAD

Major city streets are a tangle of smoke spewing *corriente* (short distance) buses and taxis. Buses and taxis stop to pick up and drop off passengers anywhere, often in the middle of the road in fast moving traffic, and are a major hazard. Some people like the adrenaline rush involved. Others opt to hire a driver or take taxis instead of driving.

Buses

Most urban Colombians use city buses as their main form of transportation. City streets are clogged with lanes of bumper-to-bumper buses that swerve in and out of traffic to get around

each other, constituting *the* major traffic hazard on city streets. Buses are full to capacity—Colombians rely on bus services every day.

Corriente buses serve fixed short distance routes, making frequent stops. Expect crowded, brightly painted, *salsa* blasting, rickety vehicles and a slow ride. There are usually no official bus stops, so buses pick up passengers anywhere, stopping in moving traffic to let people on and off. To catch the bus, wave your arms in the air and the driver will pull over to pick you up. Signs displayed in the windshield state the route and main destinations, but are difficult to understand and a mystery even to locals. The best method to figure out what bus you should take is to simply ask the driver if he passes by your destination. (*"Pasa usted por* [your destination]? *"*)

The safest way to make a long trip is to fly—long-distance bus travel is not recommended.

The TransMilenio

Bogotá's ultramodern TransMilenio bus system functions like an aboveground metro, running on dedicated road lanes and stopping at designated "stations" along specified routes. Begun in 2001 and still expanding, the TransMilenio has improved city transit greatly. Bogotanos see their TransMilenio as a positive symbol of their modern city, an archetype of contemporary urban design. Buses are clean and comfortable, but crowded (cramped standing room only) at rush hour, which provides easy opportunities for pickpockets, so use caution.

Taxis

The easiest way to move around Colombia's major cities is by taxi. Only take radio taxis (a taxi that is called specifically for you); although Colombians do it, you should *never* hail a cab off the street. As in other Latin American countries, crimes involving "*libre*" (unlicensed and roaming) taxis are not uncommon. But incidents of crimes involving safe and reliable radio taxis are rare. Your *portero,* hotel concierge, or restaurant will call a taxi for you. This ensures that you are a documented fare with a licensed, authorized taxi. Drivers should display their credentials (a laminated card that usually hangs on the back of the front passenger seat), which include a photo ID with their license number. When a cab is ordered for you, you will be given two confirmation numbers. One is the *codigo* (a two-digit number code); the other is the *placa* (license plate number). When the taxi arrives you must confirm the *placa* (license plate number), and the driver will ask you to confirm the *codigo*. If someone calls the taxi for you they should give you a slip of paper with the license and *codigo* written for you. These extra security measures ensure you are in the correct taxi and the taxi has picked up the correct fare. Taxis are easily contracted by the hour at affordable prices.

> ### TAXIS: OBEY THESE INSTRUCTIONS
>
> So, remember, never get into a street taxi or a taxi that has other passengers in it, as this could be part of a plot to harm you. Trust your instincts— always get out of a taxi that makes you feel uneasy.
>
> A common taxi related crime is the *paseo millionario*, where the taxi driver picks up the passenger, diverts from the route, is met by accomplices, who then drive the victim to ATM machines around the city making the victim withdraw money from different ATMs all night long, often beating them along the way.
>
> If you do happen to get into a compromised situation, always remember that criminals in Colombia are generally ruthless and armed, so never resist or fight back.

DRIVING

Driving in Colombia's major cities can be maddening, but to what extent is a matter of perspective. Urban drivers are relentless and pushy, never yielding to incoming traffic, which often leads to gridlock. But drivers have quick reflexes and know how to anticipate the crazy moves other drivers make. Bogotá is not the worst driving city in the world, but it's pretty bad.

For the most part, city driving is a jumbled, confused mess. Cars, motorcycles, buses, and taxis compete fiercely for road space, but with traffic so jammed, it's hard to pick up dangerous speed. If you are going to drive in Colombia you need to be both calm and aggressive; timid or nervous drivers are better off calling a taxi.

Colombian drivers change lanes constantly without signaling, trying to avoid stopped buses and taxis. SUVs squeeze into space that would only fit a Mini, often coming within a hair of clipping your front bumper. Lanes are clearly painted on the road but ignored by all. Drivers edge out into traffic, bravely nosing their way into moving lanes. Buses and taxis weave in and out at fast speeds, always threatening an accident. Trying not to hit all of the motorcyclists on the road, who also dart in and out of traffic, is a real challenge; you will most certainly witness motorcycle involved accidents if you stay in Bogotá for any time at all. Motorists make left turns from the far right lane, and vice versa, so you have to be aware and think ahead. When traffic comes to an inexplicable halt, be patient; odds are it is either a bus stopped in the middle of the street with a flat tire, or a horse cart trotting down the center lane.

Colombian drivers speak to each other by honking their horns, more as a means of communication than aggression. And this is necessary because of faulty traffic light placement. Traffic signals are set directly overhead, and are difficult to see while stopped at the light. To alert the head of the line that the light has changed, drivers honk their horns. Therefore, drivers honk every time a signal changes, which makes for very loud intersections, something to keep in mind when evaluating apartments (does the master bedroom open onto an intersection with a signal?) or when choosing a hotel room.

Traffic Rules

Colombians obey traffic rules up to a point, and tend to respect the traffic police, as they strictly enforce traffic rules and do not generally take bribes. Drivers stop at red lights and stop signs during the day and the early evening, when traffic is the heaviest. But late at night and early in the morning, when streets are empty, drivers run red lights and jump the greens, so be very careful. Often people will honk their horn to alert drivers of their presence and to prevent collisions. Drivers do illegal maneuvers when it serves them: reversing down one-way streets or making illegal U-turns when necessary. Double parking in "no parking" zones during rush hour is a common and frustrating occurrence.

When there is a traffic accident, all parties must leave their cars exactly as they ended up from the accident, usually in the middle of the road, blocking traffic, until the police arrive to take a detailed report. Drunk driving is punished severely. Colombia has a no tolerance policy that is strictly enforced, which means you cannot have one drink and get behind the wheel. If you are pulled over and have had just one drink, you will be given a ticket. If you are involved in an accident and have had anything at all to drink, you will be arrested. With these strict laws, it is better to play it safe and take a cab to dinner. Traffic police are taken very seriously. Do not, under any circumstances, offer a bribe to a policeman to make a traffic violation "go away." You will probably end up in jail.

Pico y Placa
An attempt to reduce congestion, Bogotá instituted the Pico y Placa (rush hour and license plate) program, which allows you to drive only on certain days of the week, determined by your license plate. Pico y Placa is enforced with gusto; if you are driving around on your no-drive day, you will get a fine.

Gasoline
Gas stations are plentiful in major cities, but sometimes are miles apart, so make sure to fill up your gas tank often. Gas companies have stations throughout urban areas. Unleaded, diesel, and ethanol fuel are sold. For unleaded, choose *corriente* (regular unleaded) or *plus* (super unleaded.) The cost of gasoline, sold by the

gallon, tends to be slightly more expensive than fuel costs in the USA.

Gas station attendants are fond of topping off the gas tank, so if you don't want gasoline flowing down the side of your car, decline when asked if you want the tank *bien lleno* (extra full.)

Rental Cars
You will find a few well-known rental companies at major airports. You will need to pay for insurance at the time of rental. An easier option is to hire a car and driver for your stay, or simply to take a taxi, whose driver can often act as your personal driver. Drivers can usually be arranged through your hotel.

Parking
Never park your car on the street, even in nicer neighborhoods. Car part theft is common in all areas as thieves tend to steal hubcaps, side mirrors, and other accessories. Always park in a private parking lot with an attendant, a *parqueadero*; these are affordable and easily found throughout major cities. Many upscale restaurants offer valet parking, which is a good option as well.

In Bogotá, parking lots require that you back in to your parking place, so that the front faces out. This makes for a difficult parking experience, often while traffic piles up behind you. Attendants say it is done for security reasons: you can make a quick exit if your car is facing out. Today it seems more like habit, but everyone does it.

WHERE TO STAY
Major cities have an ample selection of luxury hotels, smaller boutique hotels, and more basic business hotels. Budget hotels offer very little, are located in questionable

areas, and should be avoided. The more upscale hotels offer (usually) a better location with more amenities, and the peace of mind of twenty-four-hour security. In chic resort towns like Cartagena you will find charming hotels housed in converted colonial homes and magnificent convents, but budget hotels are hard to find. In big cities noise can be an issue, so make sure to check the proximity of your room to the street before you settle in.

In smaller towns, the selection dwindles to small family run hotels with basic services, often the only (but not necessarily a bad) choice. In Monguí, a colonial, cobblestone town in the department of Boyacá, there is only one hotel. In the countryside surrounding Bogotá, in towns from Anapoima to Villa de Leyva, you will find lovely country estate hotels in bucolic settings as well as privately owned *fincas* for rent.

Scattered around major cities and on the outskirts of town you will find "love hotels," not to be confused with motels as you know them. You will tell immediately from the sign, usually hearts and neon, with a name like *Hotel Eros* or *La Cita de Amor*. Rooms are rented by the hour, and you can figure out the rest.

HOTEL CATEGORIES

Hotel Boutique or Design Hotel Small luxury hotel with well appointed chic rooms, specialized services, restaurant, often offering extra services like spa treatments

Hostel Smaller bare-boned hotels with few to no services, but sometimes offer good location at a low price. Backpackers frequent these establishments.

Hospedería or Posada A small country inn, often a colonial house converted into a small hotel with smaller but often charming accommodations. If there is a restaurant they often serve breakfast only.

Hostelería or Hacienda A larger and more luxurious inn, converted country estate, ranch, or farm, with many services.

Finca/Casa Campestre Privately owned country estates that can be rented by the weekend or by the week. Most come with an empleada.

HEALTH MATTERS

Private health care in Colombia's major cities is very good. Both public and private hospitals exist and offer varying degrees of care. Private hospitals are staffed with many US trained, English-speaking doctors, and provide the most up-to-date technology and first-rate care. You will find a good network of specialized doctors and pediatricians if you require one. Many doctors will make house calls, for around the same price you would pay for a clinic visit.

In rural areas health care diminishes greatly, with some areas served only by small, understaffed clinics. In an effort to improve health care in rural areas, Colombian medical students are required to complete one year of service in a rural clinic, the *servicio rural,* as part of their residency. If you fall seriously ill in a rural area, evacuation to Bogotá for treatment is recommended.

If you go to the doctor, you must pay for the appointment in cash at the time of your visit. You will have to submit the paperwork to your insurance company for reimbursement, so ask for a *factura* (receipt.) If you are admitted to the hospital, you will have to provide cash or credit card at the time of admission, so make sure you have access to cash or a credit card if something should happen. Travelers to Colombia should definitely purchase travel insurance. Make sure the policy you purchase covers the specific itinerary of your trip, including air evacuation if necessary.

In major cities you will find numerous pharmacies *(drogerías),* many of which offer home delivery *(domicilios).* Supermarkets and mini-markets often have pharmacies inside, while there are many freestanding pharmacies throughout major cities, sometimes one every few blocks. Do bring prescription medicines you take regularly with you, including allergy medicines, as some brands are not available in Colombia. Any traveler in Colombia should carry a good first aid kit, including hydration packets and DEET insect repellent.

Most urban areas in Colombia are blessed with potable tap water, with only a few exceptions. Tap water in Bogotá is considered safe to drink, to use for cooking, and for cleaning vegetables, without the need for any treatment procedures. Yet, many people opt to drink bottled water to be safe. In rural areas tap water is often not potable.

Colombia's sun burns, so make sure to wear sunscreen every time you go outside. At Bogotá's high altitude, the sun is even stronger, even on a cloudy day. In Bogotá, women often carry umbrellas to shield themselves, not from the sun but the burning rays.

Vaccinations

Visitors to Colombia are not required to have any specific vaccinations, but check the recommendations of the Center for Disease Control and Prevention. Of course, check with a specialist in travel medicine about specifics pertaining to your itinerary and your personal health requirements.

Travelers should be up-to-date on their routine vaccinations like polio, varicella—chickenpox, MMR—measles/mumps/rubella, DTP—diphtheria/tetanus/pertussis as well.

Yellow fever, malaria, and dengue fever continue to be problems in certain areas.

PROTECT YOURSELF FROM INSECT BITES
- Wear long sleeved shirt, and pants, and a hat.
- Remain inside in well-screened or air-conditioned room at peak insect biting times, dusk and dawn.
- Use 30–50 percent DEET insect repellent. (Check with your doctor about safe insect repellents to use on infants and young children.)
- Sleep in air-conditioned, well-screened rooms under a mosquito net.
- Treat rooms and mosquito netting with appropriate and safe mosquito sprays.

Altitude Sickness

Many parts of Colombia are high altitude, including its capital Bogotá, which sits at 8,661 feet (2,640 m). It is recommended to take it easy for the first few days in Bogotá to acclimate to the altitude. Symptoms of altitude sickness include nausea, headache, moderate dehydration, tiredness, and sleeplessness. If symptoms persist you should seek medical attention. Avoid drinking alcohol while your body adjusts as alcohol consumption

contributes to dehydration and will give you the added
pleasure of a severe hangover the next day.

SAFETY
As we have seen, even though most urban areas in
Colombia have become safer in recent years, many rural
areas are still affected by ongoing violence. The many parts
of Colombia that are remote and difficult to access have
witnessed a proliferation of illegal activities. Although
much of the violence of the armed conflict and the drug
war has been forced out of major cities, violence and
kidnappings perpetrated by criminal bands, drug
trafficking, as well as continued fighting and terrorist
attacks, continue to occur in many parts of the country,
and guerrilla and paramilitary strongholds still remain.

HOT SPOTS TO AVOID
Hot spots of violence and illegal activity include,
but are not limited to, the departments of Bolivar,
Norte de Santander, Meta, Nariño, Tolima, Cauca,
Putumayo, Guaviare, Valle de Cauca, Antioquia, the
Distrito Capital of Bogotá, and Huila, the birthplace
of the FARC.
   Areas along the Ecuadorian and Venezuelan
borders are continually affected.
   You should contact your embassy for a list of
current no-go zones.

If you stay clear of hot spots, you really can have a
wonderful experience in Colombia. Some regions have
been spared violence. Ask the locals about security issues
before you venture off somewhere—they know the latest
news. Locals will often look out for you, so before you slip

into a ramshackle shop or cut through a back alley, watch to see if their reactions indicate that it is a bad idea.

Use extreme caution hiking, or don't hike at all. Don't wonder off the beaten path, and pay attention to signs and warnings indicating the presence of *minas antipersonnel* (land mines), since unexploded land mines are a major problem throughout Colombia's rural areas, particularly in Antioquia, Meta, and Caquetá. Kidnapping is still a concern in guerilla territory, especially in the southern departments.

As we have seen, homosexuality is not widely accepted in Colombia, and violence against homosexuals afflicts both urban and rural areas. Gay travelers should keep this in mind when planning their itinerary, and consider sticking to cosmopolitan urban areas where homosexuality is more tolerated.

Of course, as in any major city, you need to be streetwise. Although many Colombians do, it is better as a traveler not to draw attention to yourself—don't wear expensive jewelry or carry a fancy handbag, and don't stray far from the tourist areas. Poorer neighborhoods in every city should be avoided, day or night.

Colombia is a beautiful and fascinating country; a visit to its sophisticated cities, Spanish colonial towns, and bucolic countryside will be a rewarding experience for both business and leisure travelers and should not be missed. And as the conflict wanes, more and more of the country will be open to the visitor.

BUSINESS BRIEFING

chapter eight

THE BUSINESS LANDSCAPE

Colombia's business landscape includes a wide range of businesses, from multinational giants to large and midsize domestic companies to local mom-and-pop shops. Over the last two decades, widespread reforms have dramatically improved the business environment, resulting in a significant increase in foreign investment, especially in the petroleum and mining sectors. As security improves and the middle class grows, foreign companies are finding appealing opportunities for investment. Many are drawn to Colombia by its well educated, competent, and hardworking middle-class workforce and the possibility of

filling high level positions with qualified Colombian nationals instead of importing staff.

Reforms have made Colombia the easiest place to do business in South America, according to the World Bank's 2010 "Ease of Doing Business Report." These reforms have simplified the process of acquiring credit, applying for construction permits, and protecting investments, although paying taxes and enforcing contracts remain difficult.

BUSINESS CULTURE

Colombia's business culture is both modern and
traditional. Many companies have adopted international
practices in order to be competitive in the global
economy, emphasizing efficiency and dependability.
Modern technologies like the Internet, e-mail, handheld
computers, and cell phones are requirements today in the
business world. In many ways, doing business in
Colombia feels similar to how it works in the USA,
something Colombians are proud to point out. At the
same time, many traditional practices such as hierarchy,
status, the importance of personal relationships and *la
palanca* (knowing people in the right places) still dictate,
to some degree, how business is done.

Hierarchy and Status

> *Donde manda capitán, no manda marinero.*
> (Where the captain commands, the sailor doesn't.)

The business culture, even as it rapidly modernizes and
adopts more US style practices, still embraces certain
Colombian formalities and traditions. Businesses are
hierarchical in structure—the board of directors at the
top, followed by the president, the general manager,
and/or the financial manager. As in all aspects of
Colombian society, status plays a prominent role. Titles
and positions are clearly delineated, and
employee responsibilities and boundaries
are clearly defined; employees do not usually
step outside their assigned role. Employees
always show deference to the boss and
outwardly acknowledge people's ranks. At the
same time, the business culture puts emphasis
on the group rather than the individual, so
bosses leading discussions take into account the

opinions of all the employees involved in a project when making decisions. In this way, businesses make decisions through consensus, causing the decision making process to move slowly.

La Palanca

For Colombians, success in the business world depends on intelligence and university degrees coupled with social standing and personal connections. As a foreigner doing business in Colombia, you should try to find a Colombian contact who can give you the proper introduction into the business community. *La palanca*, knowing people in the right places, is essential.

Lacking true Colombian connections, many foreign businesses join Colombian business associations, which can put them in touch with the right people. These include the CEA (Consejo de Empresas Americanas/Council of American Companies; AMCHAM (Cámara de Comercio Colombo Americano/Colombian American Chamber of Commerce; and ANDI (Asociación Nacional de Empresarios de Colombia/National Association of Colombian Businesses.

Protocol and Bureaucracy

Even as businesses modernize, protocol and bureaucracy still dictate the functioning of the business world. Colombian workers rely heavily on protocol—the way things have always been done. Workers stay within their job descriptions, resist change, and do not easily alter steps in a process. They are rule followers, and if what you are asking them to do is outside the normal procedure, you will probably hear, "It cannot be done." Remember, what you have requested might deviate from how things are *usually* done, in which case you will have to rethink your approach. Recognizing this, along with being patient, can help prevent misunderstandings and frustration.

While a certain level of bureaucracy exists when dealing with private companies, bureaucracy absolutely weighs down transactions with the public sector. Although the Colombian government has simplified the process, paying taxes and acquiring building permits continue to be extremely complicated and time-consuming tasks.

DOING BUSINESS WITH COLOMBIANS

Colombian businesspeople, especially in urban areas, are savvy, worldly, refined, and impeccably dressed. Cultural sophistication and attention to detail is valued, and first impressions count. In Antioquia, northwest of Bogotá, businessmen are known to be savvy entrepreneurs who "will even sell you a hole in the ground," and are so effective that they have mostly cornered the market, making it difficult for foreigners and even nonlocal Colombians to break into business there.

Colombians like foreigners and are eager to do business with them. You will be given a warm reception and every attempt will be made to make you comfortable. Most businesspeople can speak English and will freely speak English with you if you do not speak Spanish.

As we shall see, Colombians communicate both directly and indirectly, using body language and indirect speech to avoid confrontation or an uncomfortable situation. Therefore, business meetings are formal and calm. It is a good idea to pay close attention to how your behavior is being interpreted by your Colombian counterparts by asking direct and indirect questions, and by watching their body language. Make sure your tone is never aggressive or confrontational, because this will damage the relationship and, therefore, the deal.

Colombians are proud of their newly adopted "on time" attitude in business dealings, and, for the most part, are arriving "on time" more than ever. As a foreigner, you will be expected to be punctual, even if your counterparts relapse into *"tiempo colombiano"* and are running late.

They value sophistication and education and will judge you on how cultured you are as well as how you present yourself. So, make sure you pay attention to personal details and appear well turned out.

The Importance of Personal Relations

Building and maintaining a good personal relationship is paramount to being successful in business in Colombia, so a lot of time is spent on small talk in an effort to build trust. In an attempt to preserve personal relationships, people avoid confrontation of any kind, and individuals are never directly criticized.

After first impressions, you will need to focus on building the relationship. Don't rush the initial introductions and small talk—don't cut to the chase. Attend any social engagements to which you are invited, as this is where relationships are sealed. And, above all, be patient—building trust takes time.

Addressing People

Colombians use three names—their first name followed by two last names: their father's surname, then their mother's surname. When greeting people, use the appropriate title followed by their paternal surname (their first last name).

Colombian Spanish, especially in Bogotá, is refined and formal. People address each other with a title followed by their paternal surname. As we have seen, you can use Señor(a) as a title, but it is even better to use a more specific title for your Colombian contacts, one that refers to their status, education, or specialty. Doctor(a) is commonly used for highly educated, professional, upper-class people in many fields, including PhD holders as well as medical doctors, businessmen and women, intellectuals and politicians—anyone "important," and indicates total respect. When possible, use a specific title such as Abogado(a) (lawyer) or Arquitecto(a) (architect) to acknowledge someone's professional achievements.

In the business world people use the formal "you" *(usted),* and you should follow their lead. Take your cue from those around you; if they begin to address you using the informal "you" *(tú),* do likewise, but more than likely you will use *usted* in business dealings, whether in meetings or in social situations. (For more on *tú* vs. *usted* see pages 153–4).

Dress Code

Colombian businesspeople dress well—stylish in a conservative way. In Bogotá, men wear well tailored dark suits, with starched white or pastel shirts and smart ties. Some men add a silk handkerchief in their suit pocket, and some wear cuff links. Women wear pant or skirt suits, almost always with high heels. To impress, you should look professional and polished.

Business Cards

Colombians exchange business cards in social as well as business settings as another way of making personal connections. The card itself and the act of exchanging it are treated with great respect. It is essential that you have your business card ready to offer, printed in English on one side and Spanish on the other.

SETTING UP A MEETING

After your formal introduction, the arranging of a meeting should be done by telephone, to consolidate the relationship. Communications over the Internet are not personal enough to build the kind of relationships necessary, at least in the beginning. Later, after you have established a certain level of familiarity and confidence, you can communicate through e-mail, but don't rely on it entirely. When setting up a meeting, try to contact higher level executives or their secretaries to be sure that your interest and intentions are conveyed to the right person. Send executives of equivalent rank to those they'll be meeting, to ensure they will be taken seriously.

MEETINGS

Colombian business meetings, especially in Bogotá, are formal affairs, balanced by the warmth and

hospitality that makes foreigners feel welcome. Most businesspeople speak English and usually will conduct meetings in English if necessary, although it is still wise to bring an interpreter.

The first meeting will take place in the Colombian company's office. The primary purpose of this meeting will be to assess your suitability as a partner, and will include a focus on relationship building. As we have seen, before getting down to business there will be a period of small talk. The first subject for discussion is usually a comprehensive security briefing in which Colombian security experts will detail the current security climate and risks involved in doing business in Colombia, after which you will make your pitch.

Meetings usually follow a fixed agenda but not a fixed time schedule. They are not rushed, so make sure your schedule is flexible, even open-ended. Show respect for your counterparts by letting them take the lead.

If the company agrees to a second meeting, it often takes place in an upscale restaurant over a long lunch. This meeting is more relaxed than the first, and provides a chance for everyone to get to know each other in a less formal setting. There will be mixed conversation covering a wide range of topics, including family and your life back home, and will include but not be dominated by talk of the business at hand. Expect a leisurely multicourse meal accompanied by wine (no hard liquor—no heavy drinking takes place). The foreign company is expected to subtly take the check. Avoid "fighting"' over the check at the table, as this is seen as confrontation; instead, leave the table and pay the bill away from the group.

You should know after two or three meetings if the Colombian company wants to go forward. If you have a third meeting, often it is to celebrate closing the deal, usually over a formal dinner at an elegant restaurant. Though note that this is not an occasion for dancing and drinking all night.

PRESENTATIONS

Colombians respond well to a nonconfrontational sensitive style that addresses the group as a whole, while paying respect to rank and status. They make great efforts to be courteous, avoid confrontation, and keep harmony among colleagues. You will be listened to politely, without interruption. Presentations should be directed to the group, while showing respect to the boss; use as many visual aids as possible. Make sure that your pitch balances hard facts with personal warmth, as a presentation heavy on facts alone can be seen as insensitive and cold.

Colombian businesspeople appreciate sophisticated and often self-deprecating humor, so you might start your presentation with an amusing anecdote about your experience in Colombia. If you make fun of yourself a bit, you will be seen as humble and personable—two positives.

NEGOTIATIONS

Negotiations will be dignified, nonconfrontational, and slow. As we have seen, Colombians avoid any sort of confrontation so that, in the event the deal falls apart, relationships are preserved intact for the future. Since Colombians put so much emphasis on building lasting personal relationships, choose your negotiation team carefully to maintain fixed personnel. Changing team members can cause delays in negotiations or break the deal altogether.

CONTRACTS

Colombian contracts are governed by the Colombian Civil Code (1873), a "civil law" or "written law" system that is a replica of Chile's Civil Code, with minor adjustments. Unlike the "common law" system in the USA and the UK, in which judicial precedents are legally binding, Colombian law follows written codes and statutes and the role of case law is reduced to a minimum.

Colombian contracts are written in either Spanish or English, depending on the parties involved. Foreign companies should employ a lawyer to represent their interests and an interpreter to clarify all contractual issues. Colombians respect contracts and, overall, companies tend to follow through with contractual obligations. The resolution of disputes, however, is a very long and expensive process. If a contract dispute arises, parties are required to go to arbitration. If arbitration fails, the case can be taken to court.

GROUP THINK: SAVING FACE AND INDIRECT SPEECH

As we have seen, in Colombian culture the group is more important than the individual. Successes are celebrated as a whole, and criticism is not directed toward a particular person. Instead, the group will take the fall for a failure, protecting the individual responsible in order to preserve harmony in the group. Direct or open criticism of an individual is avoided at all cost in order to preserve good personal relationships.

Colombians often use indirect speech to avoid confrontation. They often don't want to let you down by saying "no" directly, so you will have to decipher indirect speech and read their body language to know how things stand. Instead of saying "no," they might say, "We will have to see," which is a good indicator that they are avoiding being direct. Similarly, you will want to take a softer, more indirect approach when working with Colombians. To avoid confrontation and direct accusations, it is better to ask, "Has it been possible that such-and-such has been done?" as opposed to "Why haven't you done such-and-such?"

WOMEN IN BUSINESS

Traditionally women were expected to stay at home and tend to their domestic duties, but today they play a major role in business and government. Colombia has a modern approach to women in business; they are respected, and many are highly successful. Women serve in high level positions, as presidents and general managers of companies, as appointed government ministers, ambassadors, and in congress. Women have been presidential candidates, and even commanders of the National Police. As a woman doing business in Colombia, you can expect to be well received and taken seriously.

chapter nine

COMMUNICATING

LANGUAGES

Spanish is the official language of Colombia, and almost everybody except remote indigenous groups speaks it as their first language. The Spanish of Bogotá is elegant and beautiful to the ear, spoken with a clear pronunciation and a refined style that is considered the purest Spanish spoken in Latin America and the closest to the Spanish spoken in Spain.

In true Latin American form, Colombians use nicknames and diminutives all the time, as much to communicate affection as to indicate a small size. If a baby is chubby or just big, he will be called *gordito* (little fatty). A *café* (coffee) is a *cafecito*, not only meaning small but meaning something favorable, and a juice is not only a *jugo* but a *juguito*. Vendors imply that their price is low by using the diminutive *pesito* (just a little *peso*). A minute more is a *minutito* but you'll hear *minutico* as well, a Colombian variation. Most measurements use metrics, but at the market meat and produce are sold by the pound; so if you ask for just one pound *(una libra),* you will here *"solamente una librita?"* ("just one little pound?")

Colombians use nicknames lovingly with each other, choosing names that indicate physical characteristics— *flaco* (skinny) or *gordo* (fatty) or *mono* (pretty and fair skinned) are common. Bad guys choose a *nom de guerre* (war name) and are usually given a nickname. As we have seen, FARC founder Pedro Marin took on the *nom de guerre* Manuel Marulanda Velez after a communist revolutionary assassinated during the La Violencia. And his followers called him "'Tirofijo" ("Sureshot"), praise for his perfect aim. Those that followed did the same.

Outside Bogotá, regional dialects take over. Costeño Spanish adopts the Caribbean sound, a bit lazy at the end of words, shortening words and slurring letters together, all of which makes it more difficult to understand until your ear becomes accustomed to it. English is spoken by upper-class Colombians in urban areas and in the medical and business world, but in general it is not widely used. In rural areas, English is not spoken at all and you will need a little Spanish to get by. Colombians will welcome any attempts at speaking Spanish, so don't be shy.

Learning Spanish

One of the oldest and most prestigious universities in Colombia, Pontificia Universidad Javeriana, offers a variety of Spanish courses for foreigners, including short- and long-term immersion programs in Bogota and Cali, as well as programs in cultural studies.

To *Tutear* or Not to *Tutear*?

Even though society is changing rapidly, and communications are becoming more casual, especially among the youth, Colombian Spanish is full of formalities that apply across the social spectrum. Colombians, for the most part, still conform to rigid language rules that dictate the way people address each other which, in some cases, are particular to Colombian Spanish. Colombians use the formal "you" *(usted)* in all formal and business transactions: the doorman, taxi, maid, your boss, and business associates. They use the more familiar "you" *(tú)* with your parents, your spouse, and your friends. But, a unique feature in Bogotano Spanish, they use *usted* with their closest friends, siblings, or spouse. In this unusual case, Bogotanos explain

COLOMBIANISMOS

Qué pena—literally, what a shame or pity, is used constantly, and on the surface it means "I am sorry," or "I am so embarrassed," or "Excuse me." But the complete phrase is *"Qué pena con usted,"* which translates as "What a pity *for you*" and doesn't really mean "I am sorry" at all. More often than not, it is anything but a sincere apology, and can mean "too bad for you," as in it is raining and you don't have an umbrella. Or it can mean "tough luck" when someone steals the parking place you had been waiting for because you weren't quick enough. *Qué pena* also can mean "sorry" as in "oops, you caught me" when someone attempting to cut in front of you in the supermarket line is challenged and shamed into going to the back of the line. American friends confess that they enjoy giving out a well deserved *qué pena*, but it's not so much fun to be on the receiving end!

Quibo Chino(a)—literally, "what's happening, Chinese

that *usted* goes beyond *tú* in familiarity. It is not uncommon for very traditional Bogotano best friends, siblings, or married couples to use *usted* with each other in this manner.

Although more and more Colombians are using the *tú* for everyone, as a visitor you should use the *usted* to be safe. Listen and take your cues from the Colombians around you. If it is appropriate to change to *tú*, you will be told or guided in conversation to do so. *"Nos tuteamos."* ("We will now use *tú* with each other.")

Indigenous Languages
Today about eighty living languages are spoken among the indigenous populations, mostly in remote areas way off the tourist map, but the number is declining. Some languages

guy/girl," a friendly greeting between friends that means "what's up, dude/chick?" *Quibo* is a shortened version of *Qué hubo?* (what happened?) and Chino has come to mean "dude," "man," "chick," or "buddy."

Listo—used constantly as a filler to mean "OK," but in another context it means "to be ready." So, *"Estoy listo. Listo?"* means "I am ready, OK?"

Chévere—slang for great, fabulous, and cool.

Darse papaya—literally, "to give oneself papaya" means to leave oneself open to ridicule, an opportunity the sharp-witted Colombians will surely exploit.

Llamar el pan pan, y el vino vino—literally, "to call the bread 'bread,' and the wine 'wine'" means to be a straight talker, to call it like it is.

Cachaco/a—a person from Bogotá, suggesting someone who is educated, well put-together, and upper class; sometimes used by people outside Bogotá in a negative way.

Rolo/a—a person from Bogotá, used by the Bogotanos.

have only a few hundred speakers, while many others have become extinct.

Speaking English

Colombia's upper class are highly educated and often attend part of their schooling in the USA or Europe, or have family living in the USA and visit frequently. As we have seen, it is the universal language in the medical community, as well as in the business community. English is recognized as the language of progress and is the language of young, hip Colombian culture. You will see funky clothing lines or restaurants and bars with names in English, and Colombian alternative rock bands playing to entirely Colombian audiences are singing in English, which is seen as supercool.

THE HAPPIEST COUNTRY IN SOUTH AMERICA

Colombians are remarkably happy people and always ready to laugh, even in the face of extreme adversity. It might seem surprising considering the hardship most people have faced but, according to the Happy Planet Index, they are among the happiest people in the world despite decades of violence.

Humor

Urban Colombians are highly educated and sharp-witted. They like smart humor, often with a political twist, and enjoy wordplay. They will turn anything into a joke, even tragedy. They are also quick to poke fun at others, so much so that, as we have seen, they have a saying that warns you not to expose yourself to ridicule, *"no darse papaya."* The long running and immensely popular television comedy variety show *Sabados Felices* appeals to the middle and lower classes, featuring stand-up comedy, political satire, and sketches that make fun of people from Colombia's different regions (and, in an immense feat of political incorrectness, in 2010 was still doing blackface in comedy skits).

At Heaven's Door

A dead man arrived in heaven and asked God, "Lord, how much time is 1,000 years for you?"

And God replied, "My son, for me that is like one second."

The man thought about it for a while and then asked Him, "And, for you, Lord, how much would a million dollars be?"

And God replied, "That would be like one penny."

The man, thinking about everything God had told him, then asked, "Lord, why don't you give me a penny?"

And God replied, "Yes, of course, in a second."

Colombians always make fun and tease each other. As we have seen, they are quick thinkers and will look for an opening to make fun and joke with you too. Colombian jokes in the city make fun of *campesinos* (peasants) and regional stereotypes. Popular humor is based on the burdens of everyday life— trouble with your wife, your mother-in-law, the law, or your family. It often features men drinking at the bar, and reflects a lot of *machismo*.

Lipstick On Your Collar

A woman, furious to find her husband at the door, his breath smelling of alcohol and with lipstick marks on his neck, said to him, "I assume you have a very good reason for showing up looking like this at 6:00 in the morning!" And he replied, "Well, yes I do. Breakfast."

Colombia's intellectual humor is political satire. A lot of popular comedy exaggerates and makes fun of regional differences, and the rest based on wordplay shared usually among male friends, and with strong sexual innuendo.

BODY LANGUAGE
Personal Space

Colombians require less personal space than Americans or Europeans, but in terms of Latin American countries they fall somewhere in the middle. In line at the supermarket a people will cozy up behind you, almost pressing on you, but rarely touch or push. Colombians often walk close enough behind you on the sidewalk to make Anglos want to look back instinctually. They will freely touch other people's babies in the stroller, grabbing their cheeks or feet. Men will walk closely side by side, often touching arms.

Colombians use direct eye contact right from the initial handshake, which is not considered aggressive or provocative, although people from lower classes are more reserved when talking to a person of a higher class, often looking down or to the side in deference.

Gestures

Colombians are not overly expressive with their arms and hands when they talk, even though conversations do get animated. Many of the same hand and arm gestures apply as in the USA—thumbs up for "great" or "yes" and down for "bad," or "no." A hand wave in traffic means "thank you," and a hand raised up and flat means "stop." The raised middle finger is not nice, and so on. A favorite is the Colombian wrist shake, with thumb tucked into the palm and the fingers and wrist thrust up and down in front of the body or down at the side. This is an exaggerated "Wowza!" which could mean "How great!" or "How terrible!" or "How expensive!" or "How delicious!" all depending on the context. Another is tapping one's elbow with the index finger of the other hand, meaning "stingy."

THE MEDIA
The Press

The written word is prized in Colombia, and has historically been the source of most people's news. Many skilled and dedicated journalists contribute to Colombia's high quality newspapers. According to Freedom House, an independent watchdog group that monitors freedom of the press around the world, even though freedom of the press is guaranteed in Colombia's 1991 constitution, it only has a "partly free" press. While the media continues to play a strong role in exposing corruption, scandal, and illegal activity, journalists are continuously harassed and targeted. The FARC and the paramilitaries have been implicated in the greatest number of threats against journalists. Although the government has instituted programs to protect journalists, their efforts are seen by human rights groups as slow and ineffective, contributing to an environment of impunity. Colombia is the most dangerous country to be a journalist in South America.

There are number of highly acclaimed Spanish-language newspapers in Colombia. *El Tiempo* is the main national daily newspaper, and it enjoys the widest distribution in the country.

El Tiempo's main competition is Colombia's oldest daily newspaper, *El Espectador,* which focuses on opinion over breaking news. It has strongly advocated democracy and freedom of the press, and criticized the atrocities of the armed conflict and government censorship. In 1986, journalist Guillermo Cano published a series of articles on drug trafficking that cost him his life —he was assassinated by a Pablo Escobar hired killer. The same year Escobar's people bombed the Bogotá office of *El Espectador.* A number of *El Espectador* contributors have been kidnapped, threatened, attacked, or forced into exile by insurgent groups or, in some cases, the government.

Semana is a well respected newsmagazine, also published in Spanish. Bogotá's English-language newspaper, the *City Paper,* focuses mostly on culture and travel, and is indispensable for interest stories on Colombia and Bogotá. See also *Colombia Reports* and *Economist* for Colombian current news in English.

Television

Radio Televisión Nacional de Colombia (RTVC) is Colombia's government-run radio-television network. Three national television channels—Canal Uno, Canal A, and Señal Colombia—broadcast a combination of national and international news, sports, *telenovelas* (soap operas), films, and cultural programming. There is no political broadcasting channel. Private channels include Caracol TV and RCN TV. Available cable channels with programming in English include HBO specific to South America, CNN, Fox News, BBC News, and A&E. Direct TV offers local New York City programming, and the Spanish language Baby TV specializes in short educational animated programs for the little ones.

Radio
While television is the main source of news and information in towns and cities, radio remains the most important source in rural areas, especially in remote communities that lack basic services. Colombia has been an international model for using privately operated community radio to educate and empower rural communities. Its first community radio station, Radio Sutatenza, was revolutionary, broadcasting cultural and educational programs that promoted literacy, community development, and self-reliance. More recently, Colombian NGOs and community radio stations have joined in a similar effort, creating SIPAZ (Communication System for Peace).

TELEPHONES
In general, many "quality of life" services in Colombia are more reliable and more accessible to more people than they are in many Latin American countries. The telecommunications sector has dramatically expanded coverage and improved efficiency since it was privatized in 1991. Today dependable telecommunications reach most people in urban areas and small towns, although they are still lacking in many more remote rural areas.

The availability of cell phones has improved communication for almost all Colombians, especially those in rural areas; today, most Colombians across the socioeconomic spectrum have cell phones. Some families even use cell phones instead of landlines as their home phones. As Internet connections become increasingly available through cell phone connections, rural Colombians are using both tools to receive and disseminate information and organize themselves politically like they have never been able to before.

Cell phone service is provided by Comcel and Movistar, among others, who offer monthly plans or prepaid minutes. For a short trip or a limited stay, prepaid minutes are convenient. You will need to purchase a compatible phone at a local dealer like Comcel, which has stores throughout Bogotá. Your phone will come with a certain number of prepaid minutes, but when they are used up, you will need to purchase a *recarga* (recharge), sold electronically from the cash register of local grocery stores.

In Colombia, dialing a cell phone number from a landline, and vice versa, can be frustrating because each requires a special code dialed before the number. Below is a list of dialing codes and instructions to make it easier.

HELP MAKING PHONE CALLS

Colombia's country code: 57

To call from landline to cell phone in Colombia:
03 + city code + phone number

To call from any city in Colombia long distance:
07 + city code + phone number

Colombian city codes:

Bogotá 1

Cali 2

Medellín 3

Barranquilla and Cartagena 5

Bucaramanga 7

Boyacá 9

Con Quien Hablo?

You may be startled at your first phone conversations with Colombians. When a Colombian calls you and you answer, the first thing they will say is not, "Hi, this is Juan," but instead will demand *"Con quien hablo?"* ("Who am I speaking to?") or *"Con quien,"* the shortened version, which to many Americans feels abrupt and rude. But don't take it personally; this is routine phone lingo in Colombia. You'll get used to it, and may soon find you're doing it yourself.

INTERNET

Internet access in Colombia has skyrocketed since 2006 and has changed the lives of many Colombians. In 2008 38.5 percent of the population was using the Internet. (In comparison, in the USA and the UK 76 percent of the population were accessing the Internet in the same period.) Internet use is heavier in urban areas, with access improving slowly in rural communities. Most users use dial-up service, but broadband is available and infrastructure and usage continues to grow.

In recent years, the Colombian government and NGOs have brought Internet access to rural communities in an effort to rebuild the social fabric in communities severely affected by the armed conflict. Their staffed community Internet centers, *telecentros,* have become a valuable communication tool for communities that do not have the most basic services like electricity or telephone.

In Bogotá, about a third of the city's telephone and Internet services are provided by EBT, Empresas Telefonicas Bogotá. Telmex is the largest of the other providers, and offers television cable and broadband Internet service bundled with telephone service for a monthly fee similar to what you would pay in the USA.

MAIL

Colombia's government-run Adpostal mail service is reliable and is the regular national and international mail service. It delivers directly to personal residences and businesses. Private companies such as FedEx, Servientrega, Envia, Deprisa, and TCC supply faster service nationally, and are frequently used by businesses to ensure overnight delivery and some supply international service as well. Colombians use Adpostal for sending letters and packages nationally and internationally, but for packages many opt to send packages *certificados* (certified) to ensure delivery to the correct addressee. The mail service is expensive by US standards. For faster delivery, utility companies use private courier services to hand deliver bills to each residence.

CONCLUSION

Colombia will surprise you. Some are stunned by its natural beauty, wildlife, dramatic landscapes, biodiversity, and untamed wilderness. Others are seduced by its sultry tropics, Caribbean beats, and vibrant nightlife. For some, it's the buzz of sophisticated cities, or the tranquillity of small towns and the country's rural charms. Even though it is impossible to overlook Colombia's violent past and so much suffering, above everything else, it is the Colombian people who impress, cheerful and dignified despite their troubles.

Colombians have been shaped by their tumultuous history—the Spanish conquest, the assassination of their hero Jorge Eliécer Gaitán, and more than forty years of armed conflict. Yet, although constrained by the traditions of a hierarchical society and the intrusive security provisions of a country that has been in a state of perpetual war, Colombians are open to meeting foreigners and will welcome you into their circles once they get to know you. If you take the time to build and nurture a relationship with them, they will treat you with overwhelming warmth and kindness.

As we have seen, family is at the center of Colombian life, while social class dictates one's place in society and supplies essential social connections. Strict hierarchy along with conservative religious and social mores govern all aspects of Colombian society, yet an element of lawlessness and rebellion rules in many areas. Wealth has never been distributed equally in this country, and social mobility is restricted by the rigid class structure. Social and economic injustice have fueled bitter division throughout its history, culminating in the intertwined conflicts that continue to trouble Colombia today—the ongoing civil war and the illegal drug trade.

Yet, after years of isolation, stagnant tourism, and weak foreign investment, things are looking up. Colombians are eager to share their country with the outside world and are welcoming tourists and foreign business; and they are making it easier to visit and do business by constantly adding to the infrastructure and simplifying procedures.

Although the violence continues, the fighting is waning in urban areas and Colombia is moving forward, healing deep wounds and working toward a more stable future. Learning about its complex history will make it easier to

understand the present situation. Spend some time here and you will fall in love with the beauty of the country and its people. Colombia is an intricate and sometimes perplexing combination of traditional and modern, urban and rural, First and Third World, rich and poor, law-abiding and lawless, religious and rebellious, refined and wild at heart—a mix of opposites that will intrigue and delight you.

Further Reading

Betancourt, Ingrid. *Until Death Do Us Part.* New York: HarperCollins, 2002.

Bowden, Mark. *Killing Pablo.* New York: Penguin Books, 2002.

Bushnell, David. *The Making of Modern Colombia.* Berkeley and Los Angeles: University of California Press, 1993.

Kirk, Robin. *More Terrible Than Death.* New York: PublicAffairs, 2003.

Lynch, John. *Simón Bolívar: A Life.* New Haven: Yale University Press, 2006.

Márquez, Gabriel García. *One Hundred Years of Solitude.* New York: Harper and Row, 1970.

Márquez, Gabriel García. *News of a Kidnapping.* New York: Penguin Books, 1996.

Márquez, Gabriel García. *Love in the Time of Cholera.* New York: Alfred A. Knopf, 1998.

Otis, John. *The Law of the Jungle.* New York: William Morrow, 2010.

Rosero, Evelio. *The Armies.* New York: New Directions Books, 2007.

Silva, Armando. *Bogotá Imaginada.* Bogotá: Distribuidora y Editora Aguilar, Altea, Taurus, Alfaguara, S.A., 2003.

In-Flight Spanish. New York: Living Language, 2001.

Spanish. A Complete Course. New York: Living Language, 2005.

Fodor's Spanish for Travelers (CD Package). New York: Living Language, 2005.

Index

Acknowledgments

My deepest gratitude to all of you who so generously shared your personal experiences and professional contacts with me, teaching me about Colombia and about myself. I could not have done it without you! Thank you to Grandpa Sidney and Grandma Bee for always telling me I could do anything; to Dad for understanding, to Tom and Illya, Sena, Elaine, and all of my family for letting me go and wanting to hear my stories. Thank you to Dashiell for sharing these wonderful days with me and making me smile. And, above all, to Michael for always believing in me, and for taking us on this amazing journey that is making our dreams come true.